The Awesome Book of Unusual Bible Heroes for Kids

Sandy Silverthorne

HARVEST HOUSE PUBLISHERS

EUGENE, OREGON

Cover by Left Coast Design, Portland, Oregon

Cover illustrations © Sandy Silverthorne

THE AWESOME BOOK OF UNUSUAL BIBLE HEROES FOR KIDS

Published by Harvest House Publishers
Eugene, Oregon 97402
www.harvesthousepublishers.com

ISBN 978-0-7369-2925-7 (pbk.)
ISBN 978-0-7369-4226-3 (eBook)

Printed in the United States of America

12 13 14 15 16 17 18 19 20 / BP-SK / 10 9 8 7 6 5 4 3 2 1

To my beautiful wife, best friend, and hero, Vicki—
thank you for always listening and laughing in all the right places.
And to Christy—what a joy and privilege it is watching you
become a beautiful and talented young woman.

To the West and Nevin families—thanks for all the memories,
laughter, and family fun.

Contents

Welcome to *The Awesome Book of Unusual Bible Heroes for Kids*!

In the beginning, God created...everything! He made the heavens and the earth, the oceans and the rivers, the stars and the planets, the mountains and the valleys, the glaciers, forests, tigers, monkeys, giraffes, and even the platypuses! But the best things God created were people.

Throughout the entire Bible we meet some pretty amazing folks—kings and queens, peasants and beggars. Some were old, and some were just kids. But they all had this in common: They were friends of God and loved and trusted Him, sometimes even when that wasn't the popular or easy thing to do.

What if you were threatened with being tossed into a fiery furnace just for worshipping God? Or what if soldiers were chasing you because you happened to be loyal to the wrong king at the wrong time? What if an angry army was headed for your house to wipe out all your friends and family? Could God use you to be the one to step in and save the day?

In *The Awesome Book of Unusual Bible Heroes for Kids,* you're going to meet some fairly unknown but amazing people. A general who goes for a swim, the world's first counterintelligence agent, a queen who risked her life to save her people, and two best friends who defeated an entire battalion!

Through these stories you're going to find that even if you aren't big or strong or rich or famous, God can do tremendous things through you. You don't even have to be in the majority. If you want to be like the people you're about to meet, you just have to be one thing—available.

So fasten your seat belt and get ready to meet some pretty amazing and unusual heroes. People with courage, wisdom, trust, and faith. But best of all, they're people just like you!

1

Special Deliveries: The Egyptian Midwives

Exodus 1

Early in their history, God's people—the Israelites—lived in Egypt for about 400 years. At first there were just a few of them, but they kept growing and growing until there were more than one million. Pharaoh, the king of Egypt, started worrying that they might rebel and take over the country. To make sure that wouldn't happen, he issued a crazy order that he hoped would weaken the Hebrew people...

"Did you hear the order from Pharaoh?" Shiphrah said. "It says that if a Jewish woman gives birth to a little boy, we're supposed to throw him in the river!"

"What! That's horrible!" said Puah. These women were midwives. Their job was to help women deliver their babies and keep them healthy.

Shiphrah handed Puah a written copy of the official order. "We can't do that!" Puah said after reading it. "What would God say?"

"I don't think He'd like it."

But Pharaoh was the king of Egypt, and his orders were to be followed—*or else*. He thought that too many Jewish people lived in his land, and he was afraid they would revolt, so he came up with his awful plan to kill all the newborn boys.

"What will we do?" one of the other midwives asked.

"Well, I don't know about you, but I'm going to obey God rather than Pharaoh," Shiphrah answered.

The other ladies agreed. "We will too. But how do we get away with it?"

Shiphrah scratched her head and thought. "I've got an idea. Mrs. Lowenstein down the block is due to have her baby any day. Watch what I do, and then you all do the same."

Sure enough, the next day Mrs. Lowenstein's 11-year-old daughter showed up at Shiphrah's house. "My mom's having the baby!" she said. "Come quick—we need your help to deliver it!"

Shiphrah and the little girl rushed down to the house where Mrs. Lowenstein lived with her husband, Herb, and their children. The midwife knelt down and spoke gently to Mrs. Lowenstein. "It's okay...here he comes...everyone's going to be just fine."

And sure enough, after a little while, Mrs. Lowenstein was holding a beautiful baby boy.

"Let's call him Obed Wan Kenherbert after his father. Or maybe just Glen," Mrs. Lowenstein said.

"He sure came quick," Shiphrah said. "Hmmm, this gives me an idea..."

That afternoon, as Shiphrah was relaxing on her veranda overlooking the Nile, a messenger from Pharaoh himself appeared on her doorstep. "Come with me," he said. As they walked, he said, "Boy, are you in trouble. You delivered a baby boy and didn't throw him in the river. Pharaoh won't be happy you disobeyed his order. I sure wouldn't want to be in your caftan."

"Whatever," Shiphrah said.

When she was escorted into Pharaoh's presence, she knelt down in honor of the famous ruler.

"What's this I hear about you not throwing the baby boy into the river as I ordered?" Pharaoh thundered. "I specifically said that if you deliver a boy, you are to throw him in."

Shiphrah took a deep breath and then began.

"Your honor—or Your Highness or whatever—I know the edict, and I know that you mean business. It's just that...well, these Hebrew women...they go into labor, and before I can even get to their houses, their babies are born!"

Just then Puah was brought in, and she confirmed what Shiphrah was saying. "Oh, she's right, Your Lordship. These kids pop out like they're in a toaster! By the time I get there, they're already dressed and in the high chair!"

"These Hebrew women give birth so quick it makes your head spin," Shiphrah agreed. "We'll try to do better—you know, throw more babies in the river—but I tell you, these kids look like they're being shot out of a cannon. One minute, labor, and the next minute—bang, zoom—there's the kid!"

Pharaoh was clearly ready for this conversation to be over. "Well, get there quicker next time," he said. "We can't have any more Hebrew boys born around here!"

"Oh yes, yes," the ladies said as they backed out and stepped into the outer hallway.

Shiphrah smiled and winked at Puah as they walked down the marble hallway leading to the street. She knew that even after their stern warning, they wouldn't throw any babies into the river. These two little-known heroes of the Old Testament wanted to honor God more than Pharaoh.

The Big Picture

Have you ever done something you believed God wanted you to do even though it wasn't the popular thing to do? Maybe you were nice to a new kid at school when no one else was talking to him or her. Or maybe you followed a rule even when none of your friends did. These midwives risked everything to follow God, and as a result, Pharaoh's plan for the destruction of the Hebrew children was frustrated.

2

Minority Report: Joshua and Caleb

Numbers 13–14

When the descendants of Israel grew into a great nation, they left Egypt and traveled to a land God promised to give them. Moses was their leader, which was probably a frustrating job because the people complained endlessly. First they were afraid they wouldn't have enough to eat. Then they needed water. One day they even decided to build and worship a golden calf! So Moses must have been really happy when they finally got close to the Promised Land.

"Finally, after two years of wandering and complaining, the people can settle in the land, and I won't have to listen to their grumbling anymore!" he thought. But what happened next not only discouraged Moses and the people but also caused them to wander in the desert for another 40 years!

Moses and all of the children of Israel were camping in the Wilderness of Paran, preparing to enter the Promised Land, when God spoke to Moses: "I want you to send some spies into the land that I'm giving you."

"Hmm, spies," thought Moses. "That sounds exciting." He called leaders of each of the 12 tribes together and talked to them.

"Okay, I need one guy from each tribe to go into the land, check it out, and come back and let us know what it's like. You know...what the cities are like, whether they've got big walls, stuff like that.

"We also need to know what the food is like. Does it grow in abundance there? And what are the people like? Will we be able to defeat them? We need to know...well, you know, the regular spy stuff."

So the 12 spies snuck across the Jordan River and into the land that God had promised to give His people. The spies did just what Moses had asked them. They checked out the cities, the people, and their weapons. But what really surprised them were the fruits and vegetables!

"Check this out!" Gaddi son of Susi shouted. "I wonder what kind of fertilizer they're using—look at these grapes! They're as big as baseballs! We'd better take some back as a sample, or nobody will believe us." So the spies cut down a grapevine. The grapes were so big and the vine was so heavy, they carried it on a pole between them. Imagine that!

The 12 spies stayed in the land for 40 days and finally crossed back over the Jordan River and returned to the people. When they arrived, Moses gathered all of the people together for what he was sure was going to be a glowing report—a delightful travelogue of the spies' trip through the Promised Land. But what he got was a huge surprise.

The spies started out great. "This place is amazing," they began, holding up the grapes and other stuff they had gathered. "Grapes the size of softballs and melons you could use in the NBA."

"Oooo, ahhh," all the people said in awe.

The spies continued. "It was fantastic! Rivers, lakes, fruits, vegetables, entrees, and milk and honey for dessert. It was amazing!"

"Oooo, ahhh," the crowd said.

"One thing, though," one of the spies said.

Moses looked over at him. "What's that?"

The spy continued. "The people we—or actually, *you*—are going to fight are really strong! They live in cities surrounded by walls that are a hundred feet high!" he exaggerated. "And they're heavily armed!"

"Oooo, ahhh—augghhh!" the people exclaimed.

"Wait, there's more," the other spies added. The crowd's eyes got bigger. "A lot of the people are...they're...well, they're..."

"Just say it!" the crowd shouted, "We can take it!"

"They're GIANTS!"

"Augghhh, GIANTS!" the crowd shouted, and they started to wail. "You never told us anything about giants!" they cried to Moses.

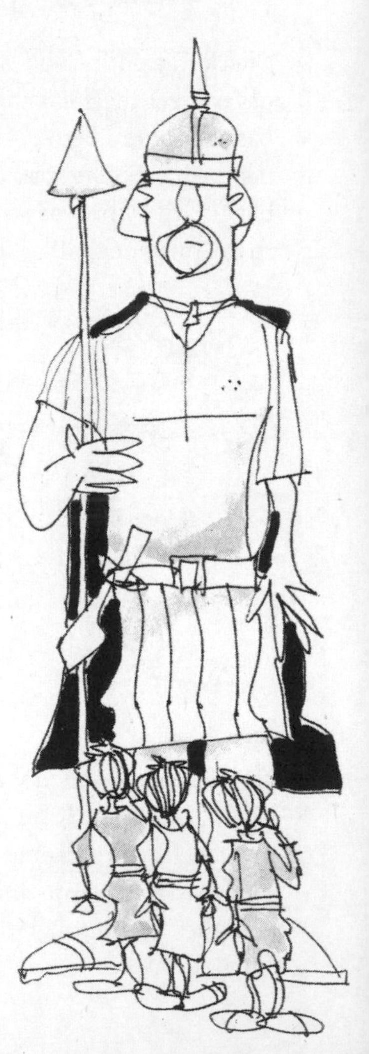

But two of the spies, Joshua and Caleb, couldn't take it anymore.

"Wait a second!" Caleb shouted. "You don't understand! Sure, the people look strong, and they've got walled cities, but with God's help, we can fight them and take over the land!"

"Hmmm," the crowd said, considering what they'd just heard. "Maybe he's right. Maybe we could do it."

"No way!" shouted one of the other spies. "We're not able to go up against these guys. They're *huge*—and *mean*!"

"And what's more," another chimed in, "the land itself eats the people who live there. Think about that! The land itself!"

"Eeewww!" all the people said, not considering that this was actually impossible.

The spy continued. "And remember the *giants*! They're everywhere! When we saw them, we felt like grasshoppers compared to them. It was bad."

The people started crying. "Oh, no—we're stuck out here in the desert, and the Promised Land is too scary to go into. What can we do? This is terrible!"

Caleb's friend Joshua jumped up on top of a big rock. "Listen, everybody, you've got to get it together! The land is awesome! And if God is with us, nothing can stand in our way. We can do this—don't be afraid!"

But the people wouldn't listen to Joshua and Caleb. They only got more scared and upset. They even got mad at Moses. "Why have you brought us out here—so we can die here in the wilderness? Oh woe is us, woe is us!"

So instead of moving forward and taking possession of the land God had promised them, the children of Israel continued to wander in the wilderness for 40 years, and that generation never got to go into the Promised Land at all—except Joshua and Caleb, that is. God rewarded those two for their trust and obedience. He let them live in the land and enjoy everything He had promised to give them. Why? Because they courageously trusted God even when everyone else disagreed with them.

The Big Picture

Joshua and Caleb had something the other spies didn't have. The other spies saw only the giants, the walls, and the other scary stuff, but these two spies saw something bigger. They knew that God wanted them to go into the land, and they also knew He would make a way for them to do it. They had faith. Yes, there were obstacles, but Joshua and Caleb knew that God was bigger and stronger than anything they could possibly face. And their faith empowered them to move forward and join with God in their mission.

3

Search and Rescue: Rahab

Joshua 2; 6

The Jewish people wandered in the wilderness for 40 years. Finally the time came for them to enter into the Promised Land under a new leader—Joshua. He was one of the spies Moses had sent into the land 40 years earlier, so Joshua thought he should send in more spies now. Their job was to learn about Jericho, the first of the cities they were to conquer. But would these spies bring a more encouraging report than the first ones did?

Joshua stood on the hillside overlooking the Jordan Valley. Off in the distance he could see the city of Jericho. It was one tough place—big walls, giant weapons, and rough-looking guards.

He called two of his most loyal soldiers. "I want you to go and spy out the land—especially the city of Jericho. That's going to be the first city we conquer after we cross the Jordan River into the Promised Land. Don't tell anyone what you're doing, but come back and report to me what you find there."

As the two soldiers left, Joshua remembered being one of the spies Moses sent into the Promised Land 40 years earlier. That hadn't turned out so good. Joshua hoped this time would be a lot better.

The two spies got up early the next morning and left the camp before sunrise. As they approached Jericho, they could see the huge walls surrounding it, the giant wooden gates at the entrance, and the big, mean-looking armed guards. The two spies gulped and looked at each other.

"Here goes," the first one said. He took a deep breath and walked toward the gates. "Try to blend in."

They explored the city, taking note of all the soldiers and their weapons and horses. Stopping in the marketplace to get something to eat, they came across a young woman named Rahab. She seemed nice enough, so they struck up a conversation.

"Could we ask you a few questions?" they said.

"Sure, come on over to my house," she said. She led them through the streets until they were finally inside her tastefully decorated home. "You're not from around here, are you?" she asked as she closed the door and looked out the window to make sure no one had followed them. The spies looked at one another.

"No, we're, uh...tourists, just out seeing the sights." Actually that was true. Only most tourists didn't make sketches, take measurements, and ask locals how many men were currently enlisted in the army. They smiled innocently.

"Oh, drop the act—I wasn't born yesterday, " she said. "I know who you are. You're Israelites from that huge army on the other side of the Jordan. Did you think we wouldn't notice you? How many of you are there—one, two million?"

"Close to two," the first spy said. "We were hoping to blend in."

"Well, everyone's talking about you," she said. "You've got us scared to death. We've heard about how God opened the Red Sea for you and how He keeps defeating your enemies."

Just then there was a knock on the door. "Rahab! We're here with orders from the king!"

"Rats," she whispered, looking around. "Quick, run to the roof!" she added as she scooted the two spies up the stairs. "There are some long stalks of flax up there. Hide under them and don't say a word. They never look under the flax." She turned back toward the door as she called out in a cheerful voice, "Coming..."

She straightened her hair and opened the door. "Sorry—I was in the shower," she said. "What can I do for you?" she asked innocently.

"Turn over the men who were here talking to you. They're secret agents from the Israelites, and they've come to spy out our city before they attack us."

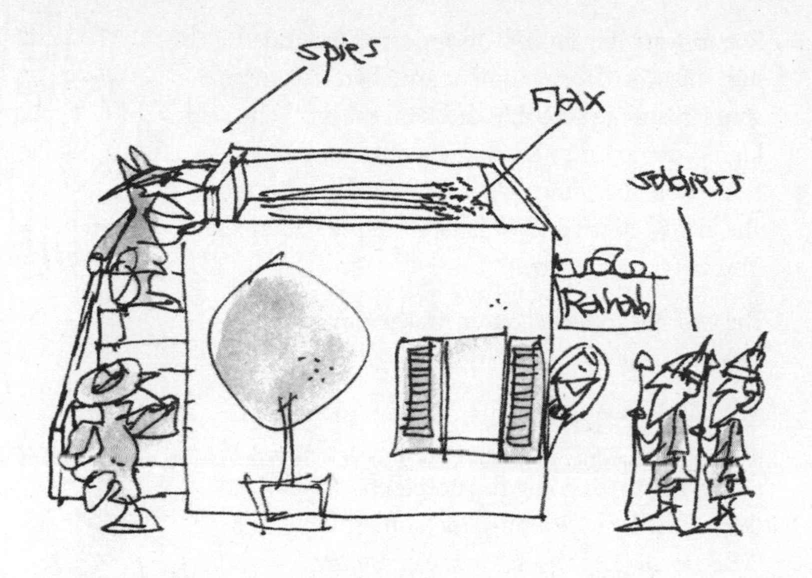

"Agents? Spies? Attack? You've been watching too much TV," Rahab said. "But come to think of it, there were two guys here. Nice kids. I had no idea who they were. They left a little before dark. They must have slipped out just as the main gate was being shut for the night." Rahab held up her thumb and forefinger. "You missed 'em by this much."

Upstairs, the two spies lay under the stalks, trying not to make any noise. "This flax is horrible for my allergies," one of them whispered.

"Shhhh!" the other one said. They could hear Rahab down below talking to the captain of the guard.

The captain looked at Rahab suspiciously. She smiled innocently and said, "If you leave right now, you'll probably be able to catch up with them," she said urgently.

The captain turned and looked at his men. "Well, what are you waiting for? Go out the gate and catch up with these guys!" They all turned and ran toward the gate.

Rahab watched as they disappeared around the corner. She waited for a moment and then walked up the stairs. "I should probably check on the flax," she said loudly. She tried to act nonchalant, but inside her heart was pounding. When she reached the roof, she leaned down and whispered to the two spies. "You can come out now!"

The two spies crawled out from their makeshift hideout. One of them sneezed.

"We all know that you're going to come and attack our city," Rahab said quietly. "And we know you're going to succeed because God is with you. Promise me something. When it all goes down, please spare my family and me. I hid you and saved your life, so will you do the same for me?"

"We promise we will," the spies answered as they brushed off the flax. "That is, if you keep our visit a secret."

"Come with me," she said as she led them over to an upstairs window. She unrolled a beautiful scarlet cord and tied it to the dresser. "I'll let you down through this opening on the wall. Go and hide in the mountains until the men who are searching for you return. You'll be safe then."

The two spies grasped the cord and rappelled down the wall to the ground below. One of them yelled up to Rahab. "Hang this scarlet

cord in the same window when we come back for the battle. That way we'll know which house is yours. Everyone who stays inside with you will be safe. We promise!"

Weeks later, the army of Israel showed up. They marched around the city once a day for six days. On the seventh day, they marched around the city seven times. Then the priests blew a long blast on trumpets, the soldiers gave out a shout, and Jericho's gigantic walls came tumbling down. There was a huge battle, and during the chaos, the two spies searched frantically through the city for the house where Rahab had hidden them.

Finally one of them looked up—there it was! The scarlet cord! They ran to the house and knocked on the door. "Rahab! It's us! The spies, remember? We're here to rescue you and your family!"

Rahab had everybody ready—her parents, brothers, sisters, and in-laws. She even had a few cats, three dogs, and a gerbil. The two spies led the whole group back to the camp of Israel, where they were warmly welcomed. Rahab and her family stayed with the Israelites from then on.

The Big Picture

God knew He was going to destroy Jericho by supernaturally knocking down the city walls, but He sent the two spies in anyway. Why did He do that? It was because He knew about a young woman and her family in the city who needed to be saved.

And isn't it cool that she used a scarlet (deep red) cord to identify where she was? God used that as a sign to point us to Jesus, who hundreds of years later willingly shed His scarlet blood to save us.

4

Losing Weight the Hard Way: Ehud and Eglon

Judges 3:12-30

WARNING!

THE FOLLOWING STORY DEPICTS GRAPHIC AND GRUESOME DETAILS THAT ONLY MALES BETWEEN THE AGES OF 8 AND 12 CAN TRULY APPRECIATE. THE EDITORS REGRET THAT GIRLS WILL PROBABLY RUN SCREAMING FROM THE ROOM WHEN THEY DISCOVER THESE GORY DETAILS. BOYS, HOWEVER, WILL ONLY BE SCREAMING FOR MORE.

Several years after the people of Israel settled in the Promised Land, Joshua died. For a long time, the people pretty much did whatever they wanted to. Unfortunately, they started falling apart—following after the gods of the Canaanites, not resting on the Sabbath, and generally treating each other pretty poorly. Whenever they got in trouble and cried out to God, He sent them a leader, who delivered them from their enemies. We call these leaders judges, but they also served as commanders of the army.

The name of one of the judges was Ehud.

The Israelites were not obeying God, so when their defenses were down, God strengthened a king in the country of Moab—right next door to Israel—and allowed him to wreak havoc on the Jews.

This king's name was Eglon, and he was *huge*.

(Can you imagine his parents choosing his name? "Oh, isn't he cute? Let's call him Eglon.")

Anyway, Eglon was mean to the people of Israel. He battled with them, took over some of their cities (including Jericho), and made them pay him to leave them alone. He was kind of like a 500-pound playground bully.

The Jewish people were practically slaves to Eglon. So they cried out to the Lord in prayer, and God heard and answered them.

God selected Ehud, a left-handed man from the tribe of Benjamin, to take care of the matter. Now, Ehud was a pretty clever guy, so he thought, "If I can take care of this Eglon character, maybe the rest of the Moabites will back off and leave us alone."

So Ehud made himself a dagger and went to visit Eglon, pretending he was going to pay the king a ransom. Because Ehud was left-handed, he hid his dagger on his right thigh. Most soldiers were right-handed and wore their weapon on their *left* thighs for easy access, so Ehud hoped no one would think of checking his right thigh at the palace security checkpoint. Fortunately, his plan worked!

Ehud was ushered up to the second floor of the palace and into the obese monarch's throne room.

"Hail, Your Hugeness," Ehud said as he laid some costly treasure at the chubby feet of the portly dictator. Then he lowered his voice. "I have a message for you, but it's a secret, so I need you to have everyone leave the room."

"Everyone leave our presence," Eglon commanded, eager to hear Ehud's secret. Everyone immediately filed out.

"This message is from God," Ehud said as he looked around and stepped closer to the king. He leaned in even closer...the king leaned toward him...and suddenly, Ehud pulled out the dagger and plunged it into Eglon's enormous belly!

Eglon was so incredibly fat, the entire dagger—it was probably 18 inches long, including the handle—completely disappeared into Eglon's gargantuan belly! It totally vanished!

Fortunately for Ehud, he got his hand out of the way just in time, so it didn't get stuck in there with the dagger. His next step was to escape from the king's palace. He locked the inside doors and went out on a balcony that overlooked Eglon's unused exercise area. He dove off the balcony, grabbed a tree limb, and swung to the ground.

Meanwhile, back inside the palace, some of Eglon's servants were wondering what was going on. They tried the door, but of course, it was locked. They figured this could only mean one thing—the king must have been in the bathroom. (Seriously! Check out Judges 3:24.)

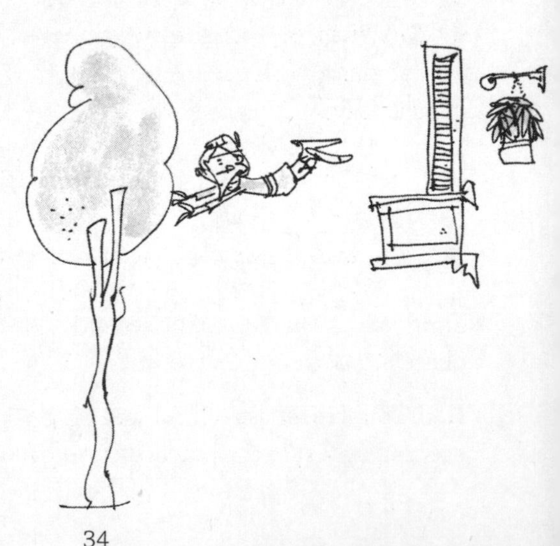

Ehud hurried back to Israel and rallied the troops. He blew a bugle made out of a ram's horn and gathered all the fighting men together.

When the Jewish people heard Ehud's incredible story about smuggling a dagger into Eglon's palace and leaving it in the king's immense stomach, they were immediately encouraged.

The Israelite soldiers rallied behind Ehud, marched out against the Moabites, and completely defeated them. More than 10,000 of Moab's soldiers were slain in the battle. For a long time after that, the Moabites left the Israelites alone—all because of Ehud's courage, his planning, his 18-inch dagger, and his willingness to stick his hand into Eglon's gigantic belly.

The Big Picture

Ehud saw that God's people needed some help, and he was willing to do whatever was necessary. He made a plan, and he then went ahead and followed through with it.

Look around you. Do you know a few people who need help? They may not be in bondage to a king with a massive stomach, but they may need someone to be a friend, to help with their homework, or maybe just to listen. You might be the one!

5

If I Had a Hammer: Deborah, Barak, and Jael

Judges 4

Eighty years after Ehud's adventure, the people of Israel once again started disobeying God, and that caused a lot of troubles. Jabin, the king of Canaan, and the captain of Jabin's army, a cruel warrior named Sisera, treated God's people like slaves and made their lives miserable for 20 years.

"This is worse than when our ancestors were in Egypt," the Jewish people cried. "O Lord God of heaven, please save us!"

So God spoke to one of the judges—a wise and faithful woman named Deborah. He revealed to her that he would empower a young Jewish warrior named Barak to fight Jabin and save God's people. The only problem was that Barak didn't know it yet.

In the Promised Land, near the city of Bethel, lived a very wise woman named Deborah. God had chosen her to be the leader (or judge) of Israel. Whenever people needed to settle a dispute, they traveled from miles around to present their case to her. (The weather must have been pretty nice, because she held court outside under a palm tree.)

One day she sent a message to Barak, the young leader of Israel's army: "God has a command for you. Gather the fighting men and defeat Sisera's army. God Himself will give you the victory."

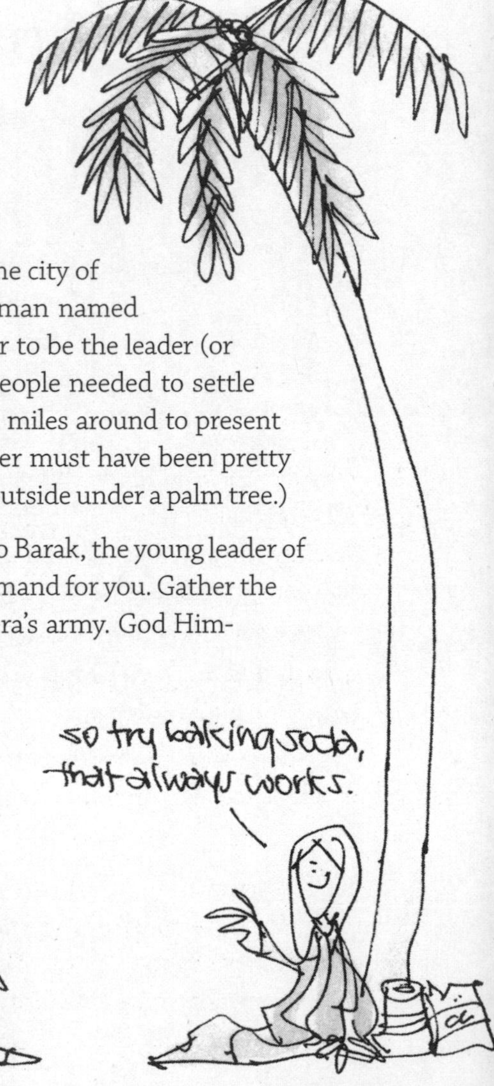

"Um...okay," Barak said nervously. "Wait—tell you what. I'll make a deal with you. I'll do it, but only if you go with me."

Deborah rolled her eyes. "Whatever," she said. "But because of the way you're going about this, you won't get credit for the victory. Instead, Sisera will be defeated by a woman."

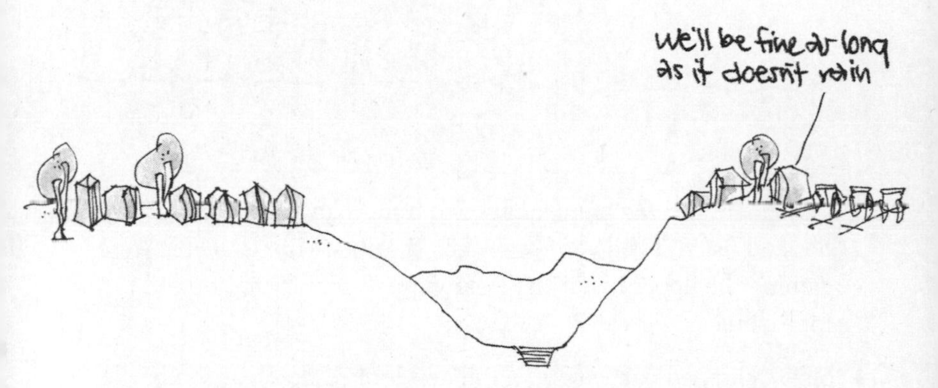

So Barak gathered Israel's army—more than 10,000 fighting men. They made a camp on Mount Tabor in northern Israel. As soon as Sisera heard that Israel was preparing for war, he gathered his even bigger army and got ready for battle. Sisera was sure he was going to be victorious against the Israelites because his army had 900 chariots. (That would be like having tanks today.)

The battle began early in the morning. Sisera was smiling with confidence as he led his troops toward the Israelites. The battle was fierce, and men were falling on every side.

The Israelite army started to fall behind, but God created a huge rainstorm and flooded the whole valley where they were fighting. Sisera's fancy chariots were so heavy, the wheels got stuck in the mud.

"Oh, great!" Sisera's men shouted to him. "Now look what you've done to us! You and your high-tech chariots!" The Israelites were gaining the upper hand, so Sisera jumped off his chariot and ran for his life!

Sisera climbed partway up a hill and looked down at the battle. Not one of his men had survived! He turned around and kept climbing until he reached a little settlement of tents. One of the people who lived there was a woman named Jael, who was secretly a friend of Israel.

"Come in—you look exhausted," she said to Sisera. He stumbled into her tent and collapsed on the floor. "Here, take this milk and rest," she said as she covered him with a blanket. "I'll stand guard here at the door to make sure no one comes looking for you."

But as soon as Sisera was asleep, she went to her husband's tool chest and picked up a hammer and a foot-long tent peg...

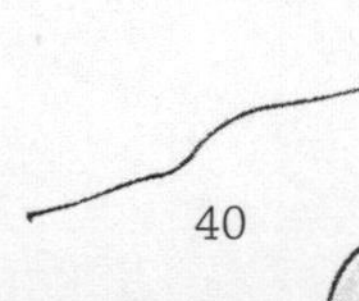

WARNING!

In the following scene,
Sisera gets what's coming to him...

Jael took the hammer and tent peg back into the tent where Sisera was sleeping, and she drove the peg right through Sisera's head so that it stuck in the ground beneath him! So he died there right in the middle of the tent.

God helped Israel win the battle that day, and this gave God's people the courage and confidence they needed to fight against King Jabin himself. Before long, they drove him completely out of the land. Once again God's people were free!

The Big Picture

Deborah, Barak, and Jael aren't as well known as Jesus, Moses, or David, but they played important roles in the Bible. And they teach us that even if we're not famous or powerful, we can still obey God and participate in the things He's doing around us.

What are some ways you can help God and serve the people around you?

6

Battle Buddies: Jonathan and His Armor Bearer

1 Samuel 14

King Saul was the very first king of Israel. He started out as a good leader, but later he stopped trusting God. His fear and pride got the best of him, and he started doing dumb stuff. And to add to his troubles, some of Israel's enemies, the Philistines, sent their army into the land to harass all the people. The situation had gotten so bad that a lot of the Israelites were hiding in caves, in holes, and behind rocks.

But Saul had a son named Jonathan who was intelligent and brave, and he trusted God with all his heart.

One day Jonathan was hanging out with a friend who was also his armor bearer. An armor bearer made sure that his master's weapons were clean and in good order. When they traveled, the armor bearer usually carried the weapons and helped prepare his master for battle. But Jonathan's armor bearer was more than just a trusted servant. As you're going to see in this story, Jonathan's armor bearer was a brave comrade, a skilled warrior, and a good friend.

One quiet, sleepy afternoon, Jonathan was playing checkers with his armor bearer. The trusted servant rarely complained, but this day he was feeling antsy. "This is boring," he said.

"Yeah," Jonathan replied. "Not much to do but play games and catch some rays."

"These Philistines are making life miserable. But we can't do anything about it," the armor bearer said. "They're just too tough and too mean."

"And there are too many of them," Jonathan added.

"Yeah. But wouldn't it be great if we could get rid of them?" the armor bearer asked.

"But how? It's not like we've got a very big army or a bunch of horses or artillery or anything," Jonathan said as he jumped one of his friend's checkers. Then suddenly, he had a flash in his eyes.

"Uh-oh," the armor bearer said. "You've got that look. What are you thinking?"

"Come on," Jonathan said as he jumped up and grabbed his sword. "Follow me."

"Anything is better than sitting here and being bored," the armor bearer said. "But shouldn't you tell your father?"

"Naw, he'd probably just say no," Jonathan said.

Pretty soon the two young warriors stood at the bottom of a huge hill. Jonathan knew that the enemy camp was up on top. Both the boys surveyed the surroundings, wondering what to do next. Jonathan finally said, "Come on, let's see if we can fight them."

"Um..." the armor bearer answered, "have you noticed that there are only two of us and that there are probably...oh, I don't know, like...a THOUSAND PHILISTINES UP ON TOP OF THIS HILL? WHAT ARE YOU THINKING!"

"Yeah, I know," Jonathan said, looking up the hillside and counting on his fingers. "That might be a bit of a challenge, but hey, if you think about it, nothing can stop God from winning a battle whether He has two thousand or just two." His armor bearer thought for a second and then smiled.

"Okay then—whatever you want to do, I'm here with you." He was a loyal friend.

"All right, let's go," Jonathan said as he started climbing up the hill.

Jonathan led the way for a little while, but then he stopped and turned around. "You know, we should probably make sure God is okay with our idea. Maybe He'll even give us a sign."

"Yeah," the armor bearer added, "because with all those guys up there, if ever we needed a miracle, it's now."

"Tell you what," Jonathan said, looking up the mountain and shielding his eyes from the sun. "When they see us, if they say, 'Stay where you are, and we'll come down to you,' that will be the sign that God is telling us something like this: 'Don't go up there. Maybe another day.' If that happens, we'll get out of there fast. But if the Philistines say, 'Come on up here,' that will be the sign that God is giving us the thumbs-up. We'll go up, and God will help us."

"Boy, I hope he's right," the armor bearer thought as he continued climbing with Jonathan.

When they got about halfway up a steep, rocky slope, Jonathan stood up so the Philistine guards could see him. "Hi, guys. What's up?" Jonathan said, waving at two sentries who guarded the camp.

The guards couldn't believe their eyes. Then they started making fun of Jonathan and his armor bearer. "Look at the scared little Hebrews coming out of their caves," the guards laughed. Then they shouted to the boys. "Come on up here if you want a fight!"

Jonathan looked at the armor bearer with wide eyes. "That's it! That's the sign! God is going to give us the victory! Follow me!"

So Jonathan and his armor bearer continued climbing up the hill toward the enemy camp. As they got closer to the top, the slope became so steep, they had to use all their rock-climbing skills. When the two boys finally reached the Philistine camp, the guards jumped on them, and the fight was on! Moments later, a few more Philistines joined the fight, and then a few more, and a few more...They just kept coming!

"There must be two thousand of them!" the armor bearer shouted as he and Jonathan used their weapons and their fists to fight them off. Then the strangest thing happened. As more and more Philistines came at Jonathan and his armor bearer, more and more of them fell before the two brave young men. It was amazing! When the rest of the enemy troops in the camp heard all the ruckus, they thought they were being attacked by a giant army, and rather than organizing their defenses, they panicked! And then, at just the right moment, God started a violent earthquake that caused the entire Philistine army to go out of their minds with fear!

So Jonathan and his armor bearer—just the two of them—defeated the whole enemy battalion that afternoon. And because of their bravery and courage, the rest of the Jewish soldiers came out of hiding and joined the battle. In fact, the Israelite army pushed the Philistines all the way back to their hometown.

It was a good thing Jonathan and his buddy got bored that afternoon and decided to do some rock climbing.

The Big Picture

Jonathan and his friend showed courage, and their courage spread to everyone in the country. Sometimes our friends and family are watching us to see how we live our lives. And when we trust God and follow His ways, they often begin to do the same.

What can you do today to show that you love God? It might be something as simple as smiling at people, complimenting them, or helping them wash their dog. Sometimes little things done for God can have big benefits. Just ask Jonathan and his armor bearer!

7

Hold Your Horses! David and Abigail

1 Samuel 25:1-42

Jonathan wasn't the only one who trusted God and helped King Saul and the Israelites defeat the Philistines. The shepherd boy David relied on God to help him defeat the giant Goliath, and that made David a national hero. Everybody loved David—including King Saul, at least at first.

But eventually Saul began to get jealous of David's popularity, and he made David's life miserable. He even tried to spear David a couple of times! So David fled from the palace and ran for his life. He had to live in the forest and in desert caves. Soon other men who were outcasts joined David, and before long, he had his own little army.

At first, David's life in the wilderness wasn't so bad. He and his men hunted and fished and built some great forts. But after a while, David began to miss his family and his best friend, Jonathan. He even missed living in the palace with the king. Hiding from King Saul in the wilderness for months on end was no fun for David and his men.

David and his men were wandering through the wilderness when they came across some shepherds who worked for a man named Nabal. This probably should have been a red flag for David—the name Nabal means "fool."

"Hey, tell you what," David said to the shepherds. "I've got 400 men here, so as long as we're out here, we can protect you and your flocks from robbers and wild animals."

"Wow, thanks!" the shepherds said. "This is like having our own bodyguards!" So for months, David's men served as sentries around Nabal's shepherds and their sheep.

Finally the time came to shear the sheep and gather their wool, so the shepherds herded their flocks back to Nabal's estate. When they arrived at the mansion, they found a huge celebration in progress. Food, entertainment, desserts, music...it was a blast!

Even David heard about the party, so he sent some of his men to Nabal to wangle an invitation. "We've helped his shepherds for months, so I'm sure he'll want to invite us," David said innocently.

"Hail, Nabal!" David's messengers shouted as they approached the sloppy host sitting on a throne he'd constructed for himself. "We're some of David's followers, and we've been protecting all of your shepherds and flocks in the wilderness outside of Carmel. Surely you've heard of David, haven't you? Well, anyway, we've been camping out for quite a while, so we wondered if you'd be willing to share some food, drinks, and supplies with us. Maybe a couple of those cupcakes?"

Nabal barely looked at them when he spoke. "Oh really? Who is this David? And why do I owe him anything?" He took another drumstick. "A lot of servants have run away from their masters. I can't be bothered feeding and clothing them!" He burped and laughed at his own cleverness. "Get out of my house!"

Well, David's men didn't expect that! They turned around and headed back to camp, where David was waiting. "We've got good news and bad news," they said.

"What's the good news?" David asked. He loved this game.

"Well, you were right—there's a huge party going on. All the food you could want, music, games...I think I even saw a piñata," one of the servants said.

"So what's the bad news?" David asked.

"We're not invited. In fact, they threw us out like yesterday's trash."

David was ticked. "What? Not invited? Thrown out? How dare this guy? We worked night and day protecting his property, and *this* is the thanks we get? That guy is toast!"

David and his warriors saddled their horses and started the short ride to Nabal's place. They were ready for a fight! "We'll slaughter every one of them!" David shouted—and he meant it.

Meanwhile, back at the party, one of Nabal's shepherds found Nabal's beautiful and wise wife, Abigail. "I think he's really done it this time," he said to her. He explained how David's men had protected them for so long and how they had just come to join the party. He told her how Nabal had treated them and thrown them out like an old newspaper.

"I know David's men," he said. "They treated us well, but they're warriors—I wouldn't want to make them mad! This isn't gonna be pretty!"

Abigail listened closely. Then, without hesitation, she spoke to the servants around her. "Quick! Get me thirty donkeys! Load them up with anything you can find! Search the pantry! Empty the refrigerator! Raid the cookie jar! We need to take every piece of food we've got to David's men—and fast!"

In minutes the donkeys were loaded with enough food to feed an army—which is a good thing, because that's what they were about to do. They had bread, drink, lamb, raisins, figs, grains, and even some of those wonderful cupcakes. Abigail left the party and snuck out the back way so no one would see her. (Hiding 30 loaded donkeys must not have been easy.)

As she came down the hill and into the wilderness, she found David and all his men—and they weren't happy. She slid off her donkey and bowed low before David.

"Time out!" she called. "Take a deep breath, everyone! Calm down! Please, this is all my fault!"

David was surprised to see this beautiful and gracious woman kneeling before him. She jumped up and gestured to the donkeys just as if she were a model on a game show. "Look at all these gifts I've brought for you and your men. Lots of meat, fruit, desserts... everything you could want, and far more than you'd get at Nabal's little party. Besides, things are pretty much winding down there anyway."

She continued, "But more importantly, see what has happened? God Himself stopped you before you could do something rash and hurt all these innocent people." She looked intently at David. "I know you're running for your life from King Saul right now, but I also know that you're going to be the next king of Israel. Don't let a foolish man like Nabal sidetrack you from what God has called you to do."

David stood for a moment. He looked back at his men and then turned and faced this impressive woman. "You're right," he said, lowering his gaze a little. "I got so mad, I could have made a huge mistake today. If God wants to punish Nabal, He can. But right now we've got more important things to do." He turned to his men. "Let's eat!"

Abigail's two servants breathed for the first time since they saw David's army. Everyone had a wonderful picnic that day right there in the wilderness. Before Abigail left, David again spoke to her and thanked her—not only for the food but also for reminding him that he could trust God in every area of his life.

Not long after Abigail got back home, Nabal had a heart attack and died. David sent word to Abigail, asking her to become his wife. So by trusting God and doing the right thing, Abigail saved her entire household from slaughter and became the king's wife.

The Big Picture

Can you believe Abigail? She faced down a whole army all by herself! But she knew if she didn't do something, a lot of people were going to get hurt. She also knew that God had more important things for David's future, and she didn't want to see him miss out by making a sudden angry mistake, so she helped him cool down.

Jesus said we could be peacemakers, and sometimes that means helping people realize they don't need to try to get even when others offend them. That's what this wise woman, Abigail, did with David.

8

From Stranger to Son: Mephibosheth

2 Samuel 9

When King Saul threatened David and threw him out of the palace, David and his best friend, King Saul's son Jonathan, met secretly to say goodbye and to make promises to each another.

"You're going to be the next king of Israel," Jonathan said to David, "and I'll be right there with you to support you."

David said, "If that comes to pass, I promise I'll take care of you and your kids and your kids' kids. Your family will be to me just like my own family."

Then David departed. That was one of the last times these two best friends ever saw each other. Years later, Jonathan and his father, King Saul, were killed in battle with the Philistines, and David did become the new king.

And he never forgot his promise to Jonathan.

King David finished his dinner, leaned back in his chair, and thought about all that God had done for him. He recalled good memories from long ago, and his mind drifted to adventures he and his good friend Jonathan had enjoyed. Suddenly, he thought of the promise he'd made to Jonathan: "When I become king, I'll take care of everyone in your family."

David immediately called to one of his servants. "Is there anyone left from the family of Saul and Jonathan that I can show kindness and gratitude to?" One of King Saul's former servants stepped forward and bowed down.

"Your Highness, I just happen to know of one of Jonathan's sons who's living in the wilderness at the house of a man named Machir. His name is Mephibosheth."

"Pardon me? Mephibo-what?" David asked.

"Mephibosheth," the servant answered. "He was only five years old when his father, Jonathan, was killed in battle. He's crippled in his feet because of an accident. He's been hiding in fear for years now."

David smiled and turned to one of his trusted advisors. "Well, we'll definitely have to give him a nickname," he said, "but quick, send someone to his house and bring him here to me!"

A few days later, in the town of Lo Debar, Mephibosheth was upstairs in his room when he got a message from downstairs. "Some men are here, and they want to see you."

"Who are they?" he asked hesitantly.

"Messengers from the king!"

"Oh no, they found me—this can't be good!" he thought. Slowly, he worked his way down the stairs. He knew that when new kings took over the country, they sometimes killed everyone who was related to the old king.

"New king—David," thought Mephibosheth. "Old king—Saul, my grandfather!" He started to sweat. "What am I going to do?" He wanted to run, but his injured feet could barely hold his weight.

The messengers came in and put their arms on his shoulders. "Get packed, Mephibosheth. You're coming with us!"

The messengers put the young man on a donkey. They traveled back toward Jerusalem and the palace where King David lived.

"This has got to be a trick," Mephibosheth thought. "They're being so nice to me so I'll cooperate, but I just know that when I see David's face, I'll be history."

When they arrived in the city, the men brought Mephibosheth before the king. David looked at the face of the young man and could see the resemblance to Jonathan, the boy's father and David's best friend.

"Mephibosheth?"

"Here it comes!" thought Mephibosheth. "They're going to behead me! Maybe I should say I'm someone else. Mephibosheth? No, my

name is Carl Shipman." But instead, he fell down on his knees and said to David, "You have found me! Here I am, your servant." (This was his way of saying, "Please don't cut off my head!")

David rose from his throne and came over to the young man. He knelt down, lifted up Mephibosheth's face, and smiled at him. "Mephibosheth, I loved your father. I would like to show you the kindness I wish I could show him. I want to restore all the land that your grandfather King Saul owed to you, but I want you to come and live here in the palace with me. I want you to eat at my table and enjoy all the privileges of living in the palace. I want you to be like a son to me."

Mephibosheth must have thought he was hearing things! Land? Table? Son?

David turned and looked at the servant who found Mephibosheth. "And I want you to serve Mephibosheth and take care of all the property I'm giving back to him. Mephibosheth has lived in fear and anonymity for all these years, but now I want him to know how much he's loved and honored."

From that day forward Mephibosheth lived with David in the palace and became just like a son to him.

The Big Picture

Mephibosheth didn't know David very well at first. He thought that if David discovered any of Saul's grandkids, he'd surely kill them. But David wasn't like other kings. He wanted to honor not only Jonathan but also Jonathan's father, King Saul.

Just as Mephibosheth was confused about David, some people are confused about our heavenly Father. Instead of running to Him and making themselves open to His goodness and blessing, they hide in fear and shame, thinking that God wants to hurt them. But just like David, we have a God who searches for us and wants to be our friend. He wants us to be His kids and enjoy all the blessings of living in close friendship with Him.

9

In His Majesty's Secret Service: Ahimaaz and Jonathan

2 Samuel 15; 17

After King Saul died, all of Israel crowned David king. David was a good leader, a savvy warrior, a wise diplomat, and a generous provider. But as King David got older, he made some mistakes. He took advantage of other people and focused on himself. When his friend Nathan pointed out his mistakes, David was truly sorry, turned from his wicked ways, and promised never to repeat his blunders. God forgave David, but the consequences of his bad choices plagued David for many years.

In fact, David's son Absalom rebelled against his father and declared himself king. Rather than fight his own son, David left the city and went into hiding. But David still had friends in the city...

"Quick! Grab what you can!" David commanded his friends and family. "We have to leave the palace immediately! Absalom is coming toward the city, and he plans to take over the kingdom!"

"Why don't we stay and fight? We will defeat them for you," some of David's mighty men declared.

"Fight? My own son?" David asked with a mixture of shock and sadness. "No, we could never do that. Besides, if we fight, the only result will be more bloodshed and more people dying. We must leave—right now!"

As they prepared to abandon the palace and escape, a tall stately man stepped out of the shadows. He was David's friend and advisor Hushai. He was saddened by all the events leading up to King David's departure.

"Wherever you go, I will follow," he said.

"No, you mustn't go with me," David answered. "Please stay here and pretend to be Absalom's friend."

"But why?" the old man asked.

"Don't you see?" David said. "You can be my spy in Absalom's court. You can tell me what he's planning to do. And any advice he gets, you can contradict. Anything he hears, you can refute. If you will do this for me, you might just help me come out of this alive."

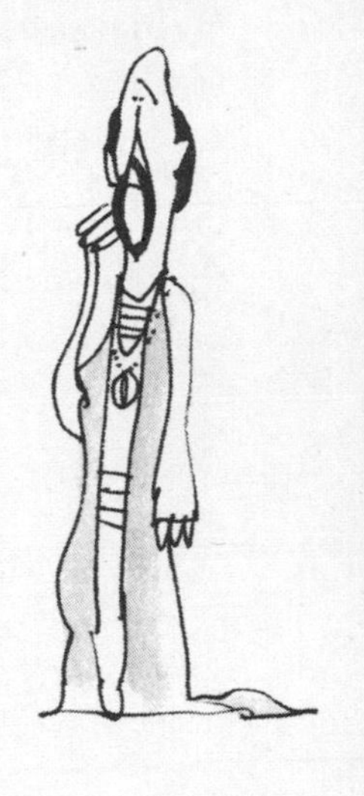

Hushai bowed low to the ground. "I will be honored to serve you in this way." He turned and disappeared into the darkness.

There were also two young boys who were loyal to King David. Their names were Ahimaaz and Jonathan. (This is a different Jonathan from King Saul's son.) Because they were so young, nobody suspected they were secretly spies for David. And they were pretty good spies at that. Can you spot them in the picture below?

After David and all his friends left the palace, they snuck out of the city and headed east toward the Kidron Valley—and not a moment too soon. Within minutes of their departure, Absalom came to the palace with his rebel followers.

Hushai, pretending to be loyal to Absalom, bowed down and greeted him. "As I was a friend to your father, now I will be your friend." Apparently Absalom bought it, because he immediately started asking Hushai for advice. And when Absalom told Hushai about his plans to capture David, Hushai sent the information to the two young spies, and they took the message to the king.

Ahimaaz and Jonathan needed to reach David without being discovered. But one night, a neighbor spotted the two of them talking to their secret contact, and this neighbor went to Absalom and told him.

"Quick," Absalom ordered his servants, "go and find these boys and bring them back to me." Ahimaaz and Jonathan were about to leave the city when they spotted Absalom's men coming their direction, searching for them.

"In here!" Ahimaaz said, pointing to a gate. The two boys ducked through and found themselves in someone's courtyard.

"What do we do now?" Jonathan asked. They looked around the courtyard, and in the middle of it, they saw a well. The two scampered over and dove in. A woman who lived in the house came over and looked in. "Can I ask what you're doing?" she inquired.

"Shhhh—we're hiding. Are you for David or for Absalom?"

"Why, King David, of course," she said. "He's the real king!"

“Then help hide us!” Ahimaaz said from the bottom of the well. “Absalom’s men are looking for us!”

The lady looked around. She disappeared for a second and then came back with some wood and a blanket. “Don’t make a sound,” she said as she used the wood to cover the opening of the well. Then she spread the blanket over the wood and covered the blanket with a pile of ground grain. Instead of looking like a well, the opening now looked just like a table where people separated wheat.

When the soldiers arrived, they found the woman pretending to be working. “Where are Ahimaaz and Jonathan?”

“I beg your pardon?”

“The two boys who were just here!” they shouted.

“Oh, those were such nice boys. I think they were collecting money for their Little League team.”

"Where did they go?" the captain asked. He was getting frustrated.

"I think they went out of the city and headed over the brook," she said, pointing in the direction of the Kidron Valley.

The men looked at her and then took off. "You go north, and we'll go south!" the captain shouted to his men as they disappeared over the ridge leading down toward the brook.

When the coast was clear, the woman removed the covering. "Hurry," she said to the soaking-wet boys as they climbed out of the well and started to dry off. "You must leave now!" She watched as they disappeared over the ridge and headed toward King David's camp. She had no idea at the time, but her small part in this story probably saved King David's life and changed the course of Israel's history.

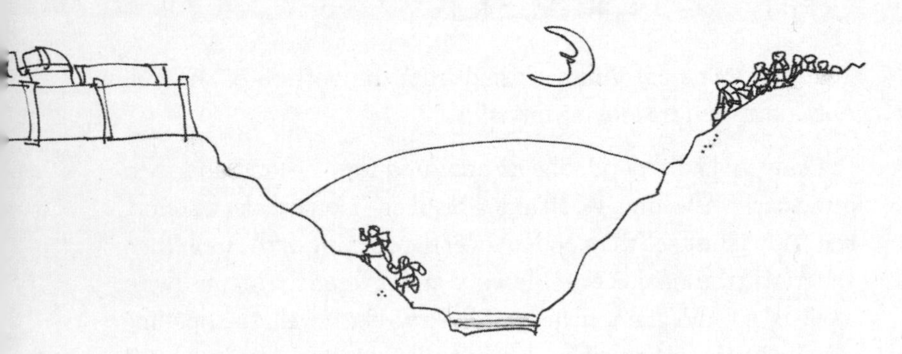

When Ahimaaz and Jonathan reached the camp, they spoke to King David. "Don't stay here," they warned the king. "Absalom's men will be coming over here to search for you."

David thanked the boys and turned to his followers. "Pack up and keep moving. We need to cross over the river before sunrise. It's the only way you'll all be safe!"

While the king and his followers took off for the desert, Ahimaaz and Jonathan headed back into the city to wait for their next assignment. Thanks to their courage and cleverness, King David and all his friends were safe.

The Big Picture

Ahimaaz and Jonathan were steadfast and loyal to the king even though that put them in danger. Sometimes it's hard to let people know that you love Jesus the King and that you want to follow Him. Kids at school and even your own friends might not understand your friendship with God and your desire to do the right thing for Him. But learn a lesson from these two kids and realize that you can be brave, stand firm, and do the right thing regardless of how old you are!

By the way, Ahimaaz wasn't done with his work. You can also find him serving the king in 2 Samuel 18:19-33.

10

Come on In—the Water's Fine! Naaman

2 Kings 5:1-19

At various times in Israel's history, God raised up prophets—men and women who spoke messages from God to all the people. With God's Spirit inside them, these servants of the Lord were often capable of doing some amazing things, such as healing people, fighting battles, and even raising people from the dead.

One of the most famous prophets was a guy named Elisha. He loved God and helped all the people. He was so famous that even people in neighboring countries heard about him and the amazing things God did through him. In fact, a military general in a neighboring country heard about Elisha and the cool stuff he did. This general paid attention because he had a big problem on his hands and needed some help.

Syria was a country right next to Israel. This nation had a big and powerful army, commanded by a man named Naaman. He was a brave, noble, and honorable man, but he suffered from the awful disease of leprosy. Leprosy started small but continued to spread on people's skin and throughout their body until they died. Naaman didn't want that to happen to him, but what could he do?

Naaman and his wife had a servant—a Jewish girl who had been captured during one of Syria's raids on Israel. Even though she was a slave in a country not her own, this little girl loved both Naaman and his wife, and she was happy living with them. Her heart broke when she thought of the way Naaman's leprosy was slowly destroying his life.

One day she couldn't keep quiet any longer and said to her mistress, "If only your husband could go to Samaria of Israel. There's a man of God there who I know could heal his leprosy." She had heard about the prophet Elisha and the miraculous things God had done through him—feeding people when there was no food around, healing people who were sick, and even raising one person from the dead!

When Naaman heard this, he immediately went to the king of Syria and got permission to travel to Samaria to find Elisha, the prophet who might be able to help him.

As Naaman and his men approached Elisha's house, one of the prophet's servants greeted them.

"Hi, guys. Say, you must be Naaman, since you're the one with the leprosy and everything. Here's the scoop. My master, Elisha, says all you have to do to get healed is head on down to the Jordan River and dip yourself seven times in the water. Apparently that should do it—the leprosy will leave you, and your skin will be young and healthy again."

Now, most people would have gone and dipped in the Jordan right

away in order to be healed. But unfortunately, Naaman was a proud man who didn't understand the simple ways of God. He was also a little insulted because Elisha just sent a servant instead of coming out to meet him in person. So Naaman got mad. "There are plenty of rivers in my country that are a lot better than this crummy little Jordan! If I could have just washed in them and been healed, I would have done it years ago!"

As he turned and started to storm away, his servants caught him. "Hey, wait a second! Think about it," one of them said. "If the prophet had asked you to climb a mountain, you would have done it, wouldn't you?"

"Of course—that would be easy," Naaman replied.

"Or what if he asked you to go and destroy all of your enemies—you'd do that too, right?"

"Of course, with pleasure. In fact, that would be kind of fun," Naaman said. He wasn't quite following what the servant was driving at.

"But look, all he's asking you to do is to take a little dip. What do you say? What can it hurt?"

Naaman thought for a second. "Yeah, I suppose I could."

"Well," the servant continued, "then why don't you just go and dip a few times—maybe *seven*—and see what happens?"

No one said a word for almost a full minute. "Okay, I'll do it," Naaman said. "But I won't be happy about it."

So even though Naaman and his servants had their doubts that this was going to work, the whole group took the long walk to the Jordan. When they arrived at the river, Naaman looked around. "Well, here goes," he said as he took off his cloak and started walking down the bank into the cool, clear water.

He lowered himself into the river. "One!" everyone on the shore shouted. He dipped again. "Two...three..." all the way up to seven. And when Naaman came out of the water after the seventh time, he was completely healed! His skin was clear, his pain was gone, and his strength had returned!

Naaman was healed in two ways that day. Of course, his body was restored—his leprosy was gone, and he felt stronger and more alive than he had in months. But something else happened that day. Because he had humbled himself and dipped in the river seven times according to the instructions Elisha had given him, his heart was healed too. Naaman was no longer the brash and proud leader of the Syrian army. He had become a humble and loving follower of the living God.

The Big Picture

Naaman almost missed out on a miracle because of his pride. Somehow he felt as if he was more important than other people, so he didn't want to go dipping in the river even if it meant getting better! Good thing he had some servants around who loved him and encouraged him to obey God and follow Elisha's instructions. It's always good to be humble and to be open to what God has to say, even if it seems too simple to do any good!

11

Chariots of Fire: Elisha and His Servant

2 Kings 6:8-23

Syria and Israel didn't always get along. Several times, the two countries went to war against each other. The next story takes place during one of these wars. But we'll find that the victory doesn't always go to the strongest or best-equipped army. Sometimes God uses a trusting servant in amazing ways!

The prophet Elisha was the first counterintelligence agent in history. Whenever the king of Syria prepared an ambush against the army of the Israelites, God told Elisha about it, and Elisha told the king of Israel. As a result, Israel's army never fell into the enemy's traps.

This drove the Syrian king crazy! "Which one of you is the mole?" he shouted to his men. "Somebody's betraying me! Who's telling my secrets to the enemy?"

"Nobody is," one of his servants said. "Here's what happens. Whenever you make a plan, even if you don't tell one other person, God knows what you're up to. Then God tells Elisha the prophet, who then tells the king of Israel...and there you go. The king of Israel knows everything you're doing."

"Well, that's simple then," the Syrian king said. "We'll capture Elisha and put him out of business. Bring him back here to me!"

The next day the king sent a huge army of soldiers, horses, and chariots to the town of Dothan, where Elisha was staying. They reached the city after dark, so all night long they spread out and surrounded the city. Their plan was to swoop down and capture the Jewish prophet as soon as the sun came up.

Early the next morning, Elisha's servant got up and went outside. What he saw out there sent chills down his spine. He ran into the house and alerted Elisha. "There's a huge army surrounding the city! Thousands of them! What shall we do?"

"Don't be afraid," the wise prophet said to his servant. "Those who are with us are a lot more than those who are with them."

The servant looked outside again. "I mean no offense," he said, "but I don't see *anybody* with us!" He wanted to cry, but he knew that wouldn't help the situation.

Elisha surveyed the Syrian army and prayed. "Lord, open my servant's eyes so he can see." And God did something amazing. He opened the servant's eyes so he could see not only the big Syrian army but also God's even bigger army—angelic warriors in chariots of fire surrounding the Syrians! And just as Elisha had said, the servant knew without even counting that God's warriors far outnumbered the enemy.

As the Syrians made their move to capture Elisha, the prophet prayed, "Lord, make them blind for a while so that I might capture them." And that's what happened. The entire army lost their eyesight and couldn't tell whether they were coming or going.

"This way," Elisha shouted to the Syrians. "I'll take you to the man you're looking for." He led the entire army over mountains, into valleys, across streams, and through cow pastures.

They kept asking, "Are we there yet?"

"Not yet—just a little while longer," Elisha answered. They walked over one final hill and into the city of Samaria, and finally Elisha said, "Okay, we're here!" Then he prayed, "Lord, open their eyes." Suddenly the Syrians could see that they were right in the middle of Israel's leading city!

"What should I do?" the king of Israel asked Elisha. "Should I kill them?"

"Don't be silly," Elisha said. "Would you kill your prisoners? Feed them—they must be starving. And after they eat, send them back to their master, the king of Syria. Maybe then they'll stop attacking us."

So the king of Israel prepared a huge feast for his enemies, the army of Syria. They had meat and bread, fruits and vegetables, rice pilaf with fresh butter, cakes and ice cream, and chocolate-chip cookies and whoopie pies. (Well, maybe they didn't have all that, but they did have a wonderful meal.) Everybody ate and drank until they were satisfied. Then Elisha and the king of Israel sent them on their way.

Elisha's plan worked. For a long, long time, the Syrians minded their own business and left the people of Israel alone.

The Big Picture

Elisha's servant must have been terrified when he saw the Syrian army surrounding his entire city, especially when he knew they had come for his master! But Elisha simply prayed that the servant's eyes would be opened so he could see what he couldn't see before. As a result, the servant saw that God's army was the biggest and strongest army in the whole world!

Elisha's servant learned something very important that day—that even though we can't see what God is doing behind the scenes to help us, we can be sure He's up to something good. Ask God to help you know what He's up to and to learn to trust Him in new ways.

12

Hard to Swallow: Jonah

Jonah 1–4

Have you ever been asked to do something you really didn't want to do? Well, that happened to one of God's Old Testament prophets, a guy named of Jonah. God asked him to preach to a bunch of people Jonah hated, so the angry prophet took off and tried to hide from God. Not a good idea. Needless to say, God found Jonah and got his attention—in a *big* way. But the cool thing about the story is that God gave Jonah a second chance to do it right. And as a result, an entire city was saved from destruction.

Sorry, Lord, I didn't quite hear You. For a minute I thought You said, 'Go preach to the people of Nineveh.'"

Jonah was a prophet, and most of the time he did a pretty good job delivering God's messages to the people. But this assignment had to be wrong. God couldn't possibly want the people of Nineveh to hear God's message. They were awful—violent, bloodthirsty, and cruel. They invented the idea of crucifying people!

"Um...sorry, Lord. I can't deliver the message for You. Nice talking to You though."

As Jonah packed his bags and headed for the harbor of Joppa on the seacoast of Israel, he had another thought. "What if I preached to them and they all listened? And what if they asked God to forgive them? And what if He did? Then they'd be my brothers and sisters! No way—I'm not going to let that happen."

"One, please," Jonah told the ticket agent at the ship.

"Where to? the agent asked.

"Away from the presence of the Lord," Jonah answered.

The agent smiled and said, "We have a ship sailing for Tarshish at three. That's pretty far away."

"Perfect," Jonah said.

The agent printed out his receipt. "Enjoy your trip," she said as she handed him his boarding pass.

"This ship doesn't go anywhere near Nineveh, does it?" he asked.

"No sir, our ships travel only on water. Nineveh is in the middle of the desert. Why do you ask?"

"Oh, no reason," Jonah said as he walked away smiling. "I think I might just get away with this."

Exhausted from his trip and from running away from the Lord, Jonah fell asleep in the bottom of the ship.

Several hours later, Jonah was awakened by the violent rocking of the ship and the sound of voices on the deck above. "Wonder what all the noise is about?" he thought. "Can't be time for the buffet dinner already."

The ship's captain ran down the stairs and found Jonah.

"What's going on?" Jonah asked the captain.

"It's a huge storm!" he answered. "Never seen anything like it! If you're a praying man, you better start now!"

Jonah followed the skipper up to the poop deck. Water was splashing in on both sides of the ship, thunder and lightning were crashing, and people were all running around screaming.

"This doesn't look good," Jonah thought.

"Skipper?" Jonah said meekly. "May I call you Skipper?"

"I prefer Captain," the captain said.

"Well, Captain, it's just..." Jonah started. "I think...well, I might know why the sea's raging and stuff right now."

The captain leaned in. "You're going to have to speak up! With all the rain and the people screaming, I'm having trouble hearing you!"

"I SAID I THINK I MIGHT KNOW WHY WE'RE IN THIS SPOT. SEE, I'M RUNNING AWAY FROM GOD RIGHT NOW, AND I THINK HE MIGHT BE TRYING TO GET MY ATTENTION!"

All the crewmen stopped screaming and stared at Jonah. "You're the reason we're going down?" they asked.

"Well, that depends. What do you mean by 'going down'?" Jonah said.

"It means we're all going to die!" they screamed. "What are we supposed to do?"

Things were getting tense on the poop deck that stormy afternoon. "Well," Jonah said, "I know this sounds odd, but I'm thinking if maybe you throw me overboard, the sea just might settle down."

"Oh, no!" The men all shook their heads. "We could never be so cruel as to throw someone overboard just in order to..." Just then a huge bolt of lightning struck less than 20 yards from the ship. "COME

ON, YOU GUYS!" they shouted, "GIVE US A HAND—LET'S SEE HOW FAR WE CAN TOSS THIS LITTLE PROPHET OVERBOARD!"

Sure enough, as soon as Jonah hit the water, the wind stopped and the sky cleared up.

"Whoa!" the captain said to his men. "I guess the little prophet was right."

Meanwhile, Jonah was sinking fast in the cold Mediterranean Sea. He was sure he was going to drown in the dark, murky water—until he spotted a huge shadow with two enormous eyes coming his way. Then he saw teeth, then a tongue, tonsils, and...*snap!* A huge fish swallowed him whole! And it stank inside! Jonah just lay

in the darkness amid everything the fish had eaten in the past few days.

"*Gross!*"

But then, in the quiet and the dark, Jonah came to his senses. "I know one thing I can do," he thought. "I can pray." So that's what he did. He prayed from the belly of the fish and told God everything. That he was sorry. That he'd like a second chance. And that the worst part of his entire misadventure was being away from the Lord. He even said he'd go and deliver God's message to the people of Nineveh. After all, they hadn't heard about God and His love and tender care.

WARNING!

THE FOLLOWING MIGHT GROSS SOME PEOPLE OUT, BUT BOYS BETWEEN THE AGES OF 8 AND 12 WILL THINK IT'S COOL.

After Jonah prayed, God decided to have a conversation with the fish He'd created. It probably went something like this:

"Hey, Great Fish, good job swallowing Jonah. Way to go!"

"Oh, is that what that was? I thought it was a six-foot plankton. So it was a guy?"

"Yeah, pretty much. Now, could you do Me a favor?"

"Sure, Lord, anything You want."

"Do you think you could barf him out?"

"Oh, finally—I was hoping You'd ask. Having an entire man in your stomach can give you some major indigestion. Here goes..."

"Hold on...could you wait until you are near the shore?"

"Oh, sure—sorry."

So that's what the fish did. He threw Jonah up on the land. *Yuk!*

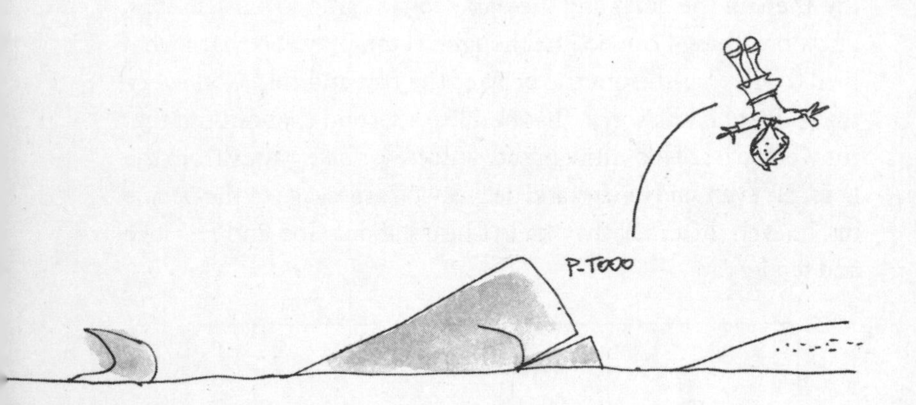

"Thanks, Great Fish!" Jonah waved. He decided to go back into the water and clean up a bit before anybody saw him.

As Jonah rinsed off the smell of fish food and sat on the beach to dry, God started the conversation again. "So, Jonah, what do you think? Are you ready to go to Nineveh and give the people a message for Me?"

"Yes, Lord," Jonah said. "No problem. Oh, and Lord? Thanks for the second chance."

So Jonah traveled all the way to Nineveh, marched through the front gate, and started preaching his sermon. It was a little different from a sermon you might hear at church.

"If you people don't get it together and turn to the Lord, this whole town is going to be wiped out! You've got 40 days—or else!"

Jonah left the city, satisfied that he had done his job. But he was also sure no one had really paid any attention to him. After all,

these people were terrible, godless, hateful, despicable, and...wait a second—what was that sound? Jonah walked back and peeked through the gates. He couldn't believe his eyes. All the people were crying and praying. Then Jonah watched the king get up on a big stage and say, "Come on, everybody, let's turn away from our evil ways! This is ridiculous—what do you say we turn to the Lord? Maybe then God won't wipe us out."

And sure enough, that's what happened! The entire city of Nineveh turned away from their evil ways and toward the Lord. And God didn't destroy them!

Jonah couldn't believe it! The city was safe and sound—but he wasn't very happy about it. So God took some time to talk to Jonah too. He said, "Jonah, can't I love and have mercy on people who are different from you? They've never heard about My love. And when they did, look at that—they listened and turned to Me!"

The Big Picture

All his life, Jonah had hated and feared the people of Nineveh. That's why he was so shocked when God asked him to preach there, that's why he didn't want to share God's message with those people, and that's why he was disappointed when the people turned to God and weren't wiped out.

Even though other people are different from us or unfamiliar, God loves them. Today, start praying for people who are different from you. Ask God to help them come to know the love of Christ in their lives. Who knows—maybe God will give you an assignment to talk to someone about Him. Don't be like Jonah and run away. Do it right the first time.

13

All You Can Eat: The Four Lepers

2 Kings 6–7

In Bible times, a strong and high wall around a city was important to keep enemies out and help the residents feel secure. When an enemy approached, everyone ran inside the walls and closed the gates in order to escape the foreign invasion.

The system usually worked well, but it had one weakness. The enemy army could close all the roads and rivers into the city, and the people inside would run out of food, supplies, and water. This is exactly what Syria did to Samaria, which at the time was the capital of Israel. After a while, everyone inside the city started to starve to death! But God had a plan to save the Israelites, and He used some very unlikely heroes to do it.

Once again the nation of Syria was at war with Israel. The king of Syria was named Ben-Hadad. (Seriously, that was his name.) He decided he'd had enough of Israel, so he sent his army to attack the city of Samaria. His army surrounded the city, completely cutting it off from any help or supplies. The food and water soon dried up, and the people started living off some pretty gross stuff.

Meanwhile, stuck inside the city was the young king of Samaria, Jehoram. Every day that went by, he got madder and madder, and he wanted to take out his anger on someone. So he sent for God's spokesman, Elisha, and threatened him. "This is all your fault! You're the reason we're starving in here!"

This didn't make any sense of course, but if you're the king, you can say whatever you want.

"Stop complaining and listen," Elisha boldly replied to the angry king. “Tomorrow at this time there will be so much food in this city, you’ll think you were at an all-you-can-eat buffet. You’ll be able to buy eight gallons of baking flour for a penny!”

“A penny?” one of the king’s officers exclaimed. “A penny isn’t worth hardly anything. How can this be?”

“You’ll see,” Elisha said confidently. Elisha didn’t know how God was going to pull this off, but he knew He would. So what did God have in mind?

Well, across town, right by the front gate of the city, sat four men. But these weren’t ordinary men. They were suffering from the terrible disease of leprosy. Because of that, they were stuck outside the front gate of the city.

One of them spoke up. “This is no good. We’re just sitting here.”

“I know, I was thinking the same thing,” another one answered. “If we go inside the city, we’ll die of starvation just like everyone else. But if we just sit here we’ll end up dying too.”

“Well, aren’t you Mr. Doom and Gloom!” the third leprous guy said to him. “What do you propose we do?”

“I’m thinking we should head over to the camp of the Syrians,” he said.

"Are you crazy? They'll kill us!"

"Well, think about it," the first one said. "We'd be no worse off than if we stay here. We could go over there with our hands up—you know, like people do when they surrender—and who knows? Maybe they'll keep us around. They might even feed us as kind of a goodwill gesture."

"Goodwill gesture? These are the *Syrians* we're talking about!" one of the others said.

"No, I think he has a good point," the fourth leper said. "Besides, what have we got to lose?"

So just as the sun was starting to set, the four of them got up and headed for the Syrians' camp. As they approached it, they noticed something odd.

"It sure is quiet over here," one of the lepers observed. "What do you suppose they're up to?"

"I don't know," another one said. "It's kind of creepy, don't you think?"

When they came closer they realized why the camp was so quiet—no one was there! Not a soldier, not a cook, no member of the marching band, no lieutenants, no sergeants, no radio operators, no nothing. The whole place was deserted! All the tents were there, all the supplies, the blankets, the trumpets, the bowls, the pots and pans...but no people!

"This is weird," one of the lepers noted. "Wonder what happened? This is like an old *Twilight Zone* episode I saw once."

What our leprous friends didn't know was that if they'd been there about a half an hour earlier, they would have seen what God did. He created the sound of chariots and horses and thousands of troops marching all around the camp—no real troops, just the sound. But when the Syrians heard what they thought were thousands of soldiers surrounding their camp, they were sure that Israel had hired armies from all around to fight against them. So the Syrians ran for their lives!

They were so scared, they didn't even pack! They just dashed out of the camp as fast as they could. By the time the four lepers showed up, nobody was left.

When the lepers realized the place was empty, they headed straight to the mess hall. They found all kinds of meat, vegetables, fruits, bread...probably even cookies, pies, pastries, and pudding. They were having the time of their lives!

"Pass the beef Wellington, please."

"Isn't this the best sweet potato pie you've ever tasted?"

"Have you tried the buffalo wings?"

Even though you're not supposed to talk with your mouth full, one of them finally said (as he took a huge bite of his banana split), "You know what? This isn't good."

"Really?" another of the lepers responded. "Mine's delicious. Try some with the pineapple."

"No, I mean what we're doing isn't good. We should be sharing with everybody else. Here we are, keeping all this good stuff to ourselves while our whole city is starving! We need to let them know."

"You know, I was thinking the same thing," one of the others said as he helped himself to another serving of meat loaf. "As soon as we finish here, we should go and tell the king about this. That's the right thing to do."

"You're right," number four said. "But can I at least finish my turnover?"

A few minutes later, they were off. They came to the king's house and knocked on the door. "Open up! You're not going to believe what happened!" the first one shouted, wiping gravy stains off his shirt. When the king's servant came to the door, they told him the whole story about the tents, the horses, the food…even the turnover.

The king thought deeply about what the lepers had just said. "This is just like that old *Twilight Zone* episode I saw once!" The four lepers looked at each other but didn't say anything.

"No," the king said, changing his mind. "It's a trap—I just know it. Don't you see? They're just trying to lure us out of the city so they can pounce on us and kill us. Here's what I'll do. I'll send some scouts out there to see if what you say is true. If they come back alive, fine. But if not, we'll know it was a trap." The king turned to his assistant. "Who's someone in the army we don't care about? Let's send him to check it out."

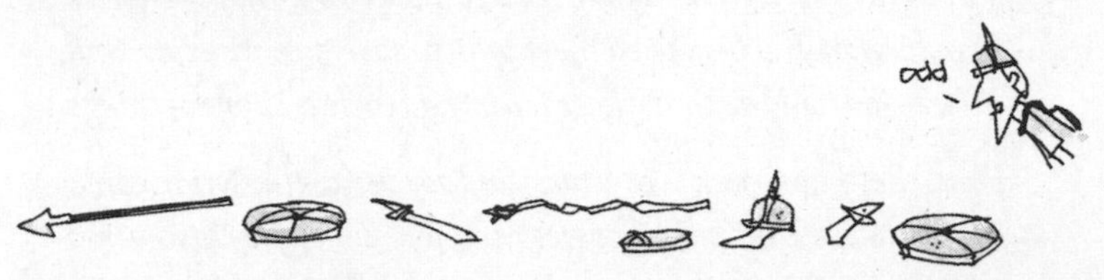

So they chose several of the most unpopular guys in the regiment to go and scout out the Syrians' camp. As they came upon the camp, they found something amazing. The entire road was littered with weapons, extra clothing, belts, swords, knives, and shields. The Syrian army had dropped everything because they were in such a hurry to escape with their lives. (Of course, we know they were running from nothing but God's sound effects.) So the scouts returned to the city and confirmed the lepers' report.

The Syrians had left more than enough food and drinks for everyone in Samaria. The people rushed out of the city and into the Syrian camp as if it were a sale at the local discount store! They brought back so much food it was like...well, as Elisha had said, an all-you-can-eat buffet. There was so much food, in fact, that eight gallons of baking flour sold for a penny (just as Elisha had predicted). God scared away the enemy, saved all the people, and provided enough food for everyone—and He did it using four of the most unlikely heroes.

The Big Picture

In Bible times, nobody thought lepers were worth much. People stayed away from them and treated them as if they were less than human. But God used these guys to save an entire city. Still, before God could do that, these lepers had to do a couple of things.

First, they had to risk everything and go over to the Syrian camp. When they left the safety of their comfort zone, they discovered that God had already prepared the way for them.

And then, they didn't keep the good news to themselves. When they realized there was enough food for the whole city, they went back and shared their discovery with everyone else.

God is continuing to do amazing things today. And sometimes He asks us to leave our comfort zone and tell people about the good news that Jesus loves them!

14

Too Hot to Handle: Shadrach, Meshach, and Abed-Nego

Daniel 3

When God's people were captured and carried away to Babylon, three young heroes continued in their steadfast devotion to God in spite of great pressure all around them. It wasn't easy for these guys, living in a foreign culture where people worshipped everything from rocks and stars to big gold statues. But even when they were threatened with becoming the main course at the Babylonian barbecue, these guys decided to risk everything and follow the true God.

"So, what are you going to do today?" some of King Nebuchadnezzar's closest advisors asked him. After all, he was king of the entire Babylonian empire, so he could pretty much do whatever he wanted.

"Well, there's something I've been thinking about for some time now," he said.

"Yes? What is it?" They were all curious.

"I'm thinking of building a ninety-foot-tall gold statue right in the middle of town. What do you guys think?"

"That sounds splendid," his advisors agreed.

So sure enough, not long after that a huge gold statue was erected right in the middle of the square for all to see. And Nebuchadnezzar was right there the day it was dedicated.

"Welcome, one and all, to the dedication of this really cool statue! It's something, isn't it?" he asked.

"Oh, it's something, all right," everyone said.

"You know what else?" the king asked.

"No, what?" the people answered.

"I'm going to have horns and flutes and harps and stuff play every so often, and when you hear them, you're all going to stop, face the statue, and bow down to it. How's that sound?"

This sounded very strange to most everybody, but because of the king's red-hot temper and his fiery furnace, nobody would disagree. They usually found it in their best interest to go along with whatever he said.

"Great idea! Love it!" they all said in unison.

So for days, horns and flutes and harps sounded regularly, and when they did, everybody bowed down obediently to the king's statue. Everybody, that is, except three Jewish boys who frankly thought it was pretty stupid to bow down to a piece of metal. *Ouch*.

These guys' names were—are you ready?—Shadrach, Meshach, and Abed-Nego. They believed there was only one God worth bowing down to—the true and living God. So whenever the horns, flutes, and harps began playing, these three just went about their normal routine. No bowing, no scraping. In fact, they didn't seem to hear the instruments at all.

This kind of flagrant disrespect got under the skin of some of the locals, who went and tattled—er, that is...they reported the boys' misdeeds to the king himself. They found him in the backyard barbecuing some spareribs.

"That's right, Your Majesty. It's like they don't even hear the horns going off. They don't bow or anything!"

"I'm sorry to hear that," the king said as he squirted more charcoal fluid on the barbecue. "I know these boys—in fact, they help me out sometimes. Obviously I can't have these three hooligans ignoring royal orders. Bring 'em in. I'll have a little talk with them and see if I can change their minds."

The next day, the angry locals dragged Shadrach, Meshach, and Abed-Nego before the king.

"What's this I hear about you disobeying my orders and not bowing down to the gods of Babylon? Don't you see it only makes sense to bow before the gods of the country you're living in? It's only right! 'When in Rome' and all that. So tell you what, when the horns go off again, just bow down like everybody else. Okay?" His face was starting to turn red. "Because if you don't do what I say, you're going to be thrown into the fiery furnace! And I'm not kidding!" The three boys knew the king was upset because they could see the veins in his neck popping out.

The three guys looked at each other and started in. "You know, we don't even really need to have this conversation, because we're not going to bow down to the statue. And if you throw us into the fiery furnace, our God can easily protect us from harm. But even if He chooses not to, we're still going to bow only to Him."

If you thought the king was enraged before, he was really steamed (pardon the pun) now!

"Heat up the furnace seven times hotter than usual!" he ordered his chief fire programmers. Nobody was quite sure how to do that, but somehow they managed to get the furnace seven times hotter than usual. Then they hog-tied Shadrach, Meshach, and Abed-Nego and tossed them in. The fire was so hot, it turned the guards who were carrying the three boys into ashes. But when the king managed to get close enough to look into the burning furnace, he saw something amazing!

He saw our heroes walking around in the fire! They were acting as if they were at someone's party, eating chips and dipping into a pool.

But wait—there was something else. Besides Shadrach, Meshach, and Abed-Nego in the furnace, King Nebuchadnezzar saw a fourth guy! "It looks like the Son of God!" he exclaimed. And it *was* the Son of God—Jesus Himself coming to protect and encourage our three heroes.

When the king saw all this, he majorly changed his tune. He brought the guys out and promoted them to be his chief advisors. He even issued a new order: "If anyone ever says anything bad against the true God, the God of Shadrach, Meshach, and Abed-Nego, he'll be cut in pieces, and his house will be burned to the ground!" Apparently the king was still stuck on this whole fire thing. But hey, at least he finally realized that the God of Shadrach, Meshach, and Abed-Nego was the Real Deal.

The Big Picture

Shadrach, Meshach, and Abed-Nego showed extreme bravery and courage as they stood up to the king and his advisors. They were willing to put their lives on the line because they believed in God and wanted to honor Him at all costs. Even though everyone else in the country followed King Nebuchadnezzar's silly rule, our three heroes stood firm and honored God.

And as a result, God honored them with His presence and protection.

15

Queen for This Day: Esther and Mordecai

Esther 3–5; 7–8

Many years after David reigned, the armies of Assyria and Babylon invaded Israel and took most of the Jewish people away as captives. In the faraway country of Persia, one of the captives, a beautiful orphan girl named Esther, was taken to the king's palace and became queen. There, she and her cousin Mordecai found themselves at the center of an intriguing and dangerous plot that involved the king and his evil advisor. It was a conspiracy to wipe out the entire Jewish race! But as Mordecai wisely observed, perhaps it was for this very moment that God had placed Esther in her position as queen. God wanted to use the young woman to fulfill His purposes and save His people from destruction.

"Queen Esther! Come quickly! Mordecai has an important message for you!" Esther left her royal chambers and ran quickly down the halls and out toward the street to meet her cousin Mordecai. He had always stayed very near since she had become queen, but it was quite unusual for him to summon Esther this way.

"What is it?" she asked. She could tell by his expression that this was very serious.

He handed her a piece of paper. As she read it he shared the grim news. "This order has gone out though all the Persian provinces. On a certain day not long from now, all the people are to attack and kill any of the Jews who live near them."

Esther's mind was spinning at the news. Why such a harsh command? How could this happen? Would she be killed if the king found out she was a Jew? Mordecai explained that the evil Haman had tricked the king into signing this dreadful edict. Haman hated Mordecai, and as a result, Haman hated all the Jewish people.

"What can we do?" Esther said, frightened.

"You're the queen. You need to talk to the king and get him to change his mind."

"How can I do that?" she said. "No one is allowed into the king's chambers without his permission. If I just barge in there, I might be executed!"

"But don't you see?" Mordecai said, looking straight into her eyes. "This might be the whole reason God made you queen. It might be for this very moment!"

Esther thought for a moment then spoke softly. "All right. I'll go in to see the king tomorrow. Have everyone pray for me."

The next day Queen Esther humbly went before the king and stood at the far end of the throne room.

When the king saw her, he welcomed her because he loved her. "What is your request?" he asked as she knelt before him.

Queen Esther replied, "Before I make my request, please join me for a banquet later today." The king gladly agreed. "One other thing," Esther said. "I'd like to invite Haman to come to the banquet so he can hear my request too."

"Of course," the king said. "I'll see you then."

Esther and her servants prepared a wonderful banquet for her guests. When the moment arrived, the doors to the Grand Hall were opened. Esther welcomed the king and evil Haman inside. She was kind but could hardly look at the man who had declared open war on her people, the Jews.

After everyone ate, the king turned to Esther and said, "Please tell me, what is your request? The suspense is driving me crazy!"

"I have only one thing to ask," the wise queen said. Both the king and Haman leaned in. "I'd like both of you to join me for another banquet tomorrow evening. Then I'll tell you my request."

Esther knew that by waiting (and giving her friends another day to pray) she'd have the king's full attention. Only then would she reveal why she had summoned him. The next day the king and evil Haman again joined Esther for a grand banquet. And again after dinner, the king turned to his beautiful wife and asked, "Okay, what is it? What is your request?"

Esther looked at Haman and began. "Well, I heard about the command for all the citizens of Persia to attack the Jewish people. But these are my brothers and sisters! I wouldn't have said anything if they were to be made your slaves, but the order says that everyone in your kingdom should go out and kill them! This is terrible. Why would there be such an order?"

The king stood up in shock. "This is unbelievable!" he said, "Who would do such a thing?"

Esther arose and pointed to Haman. "It's him! Haman is the one!"

The king was so mad that he stormed out of the room, knowing he'd been tricked into signing this order. As soon as he was out of the room, Haman fell down on the couch next to Esther and began begging for his life. This didn't look too good when the king came back suddenly.

"And another thing..." the king started. He stopped short. "What's this, Haman? First you want to kill all the Jewish people, and now you're flopping down next to the queen? Are you out of your mind?" The king turned to his servants. "Go take care of him!" The servants took Haman out and hanged him.

Later, Mordecai and Esther met with the king and told him the whole story. He agreed to write a new order stating that the Jewish people should fight back if anyone attacks them. And when the day came, the Jews won a great victory! The people celebrated and praised Queen Esther and her cousin Mordecai for their care, courage, and wisdom. They saved the Jews!

The Big Picture

Mordecai challenged Esther by saying that God may have put her in a position of authority for this very moment so she could save her people, the Jews. God often puts people He trusts in certain positions so that they can reveal Him to others. If you're a class officer or are on a team or have certain gifts or talents, God may want to use you to be a blessing to others. Ask Him to show you how.

16

Will That Be 5000 for Lunch? The Boy with the Snacks

John 6:1-14

When Jesus began His public ministry, He often attracted crowds of thousands of people. They wanted to hear His words, see His miracles, and experience His love.

One day Jesus hiked up onto a mountain overlooking the Sea of Galilee. There He sat in the warm sunshine, teaching His disciples about the kingdom of God. As He was speaking, He looked up and saw a huge crowd of people coming His way. He knew they'd be hungry, but how would He feed such a large group all the way out here on the mountainside? Jesus had a plan, and His disciples were about to find out that they had a part to play.

"Whoa, look at that," Jesus said as hundreds of people started to gather around Him and His disciples. He turned to His friend Philip and said, "What are you going to do to feed all these people?"

"What am *I* going to do?" Philip asked. As the crowd got closer and started to surround them, Philip looked around and panicked. "Even if we had a year's salary, we couldn't feed this many!"

Just then Andrew, Peter's brother, walked up. "There's a little kid here who brought five loaves of bread and two fish for his lunch, but that's never going to feed all these people!"

Jesus didn't respond but instead said, "Have everybody sit down on the grass."

Philip and Andrew looked at each other and shrugged. It took about ten minutes to get everyone seated in groups because there were about 5000 men and many more women and kids.

Jesus turned to the little boy with the fish and bread in a little basket. "Follow me," Jesus said with a warm smile to the boy.

Jesus walked around and looked at the crowd, and the boy followed Him. Was He counting the people? Was He worrying how He was going to feed all these people? "No," the boy thought, "He's just enjoying looking at all these precious people who have taken the time and energy to follow Him out here."

Jesus turned and smiled at the little boy. "Okay, bring your lunch here."

The little boy scurried over to his new best friend. "Here, sir," he said, lifting up the basket to Jesus.

Jesus took it from him and looked up to heaven, praising God and saying, "Thank You, Father, for all these good gifts." Then Jesus called to the disciples. "Here, take this and give it to all the people. Make sure everyone has enough."

For the next hour or so, the disciples gave the fish and bread to everyone who was there. Every time they handed out some food, they returned to the basket and found even more. Nobody asked where it came from—they just did their part.

Everyone ate and ate and had a wonderful time together. When everybody had eaten their fill, Jesus called out to His disciples again. "Go gather up all the leftovers," He said. "Make sure none of it is wasted." So they went out and gathered what was left, and each of the 12 disciples gathered up a full basket—12 baskets of leftovers in all!

So the little boy who willingly shared his food saw his little lunch turn into a tremendous banquet!

The Big Picture

This little boy was just like you and me. He might have thought, "If I give away my lunch, that means I won't have any!" He could have said to Jesus, "Here, take one fish and two loaves. That way I'll still have plenty for myself." But he didn't. Something about Jesus helped the boy trust Him completely. He knew that regardless of what happened, giving everything to Jesus was the safest and best thing to do. So he gave his entire lunch to the Master. And as a result, Jesus fed thousands of people—and the little boy got plenty too!

17

Riding the Waves: Peter

Matthew 14:22-33

Peter was one of Jesus' closest disciples. He loved Jesus with all his heart, but like most of us, Peter sometimes made some pretty big mistakes. Sometimes he said the wrong thing, did the wrong thing, or ended up in a mess that only God could get him out of. But on this particular day, Peter tried something that no one else had ever done. And as a result, Peter started to realize that Jesus was not only his friend but also the God of the universe.

Jesus' 12 disciples were amazed that He was able to feed thousands of people with just five little loaves of bread and two fish. "How did He do that? This guy is amazing!" they said to one another.

As they walked down the hill and reached the shore of the Sea of Galilee, Jesus pointed to a boat sitting on the shore. "You guys get in the boat and row over to the other side of the lake." The disciples hesitated—they wanted to stay with Jesus. "Go ahead," He assured them, "I'll see you on the other side."

As the disciples pushed out into the water and started rowing, Jesus turned around and hiked back up the hill to spend some time with His heavenly Father. He sat down, and even though He prayed for hours, He never lost sight of the little boat carrying His friends.

As the sun set, the wind started to blow hard, making it difficult for the disciples to row the boat. The waves grew larger, tossing the tiny boat up and down. In a matter of minutes, a big storm had developed all around them. Even though most of the disciples had grown up as fishermen on this sea, this was one of the worst storms they'd ever seen. They were getting scared...and seasick! Were they going to make it out of this alive?

From the top of the mountain, Jesus saw their distress and decided to go out to them and do what only He could do. No other boats were around, and Jesus really wanted to reach His friends, so He decided to walk out to them on top of the water!

(When you think about it, Jesus is God, and He created the whole world, so walking on water was probably not a big deal for Him.)

As Jesus got close to the boat, one of the disciples looked up and spotted Him. "Oh no!" he shouted. "It's a ghost! As if things weren't bad enough! He's come to get us because we're all going to die in the storm!"

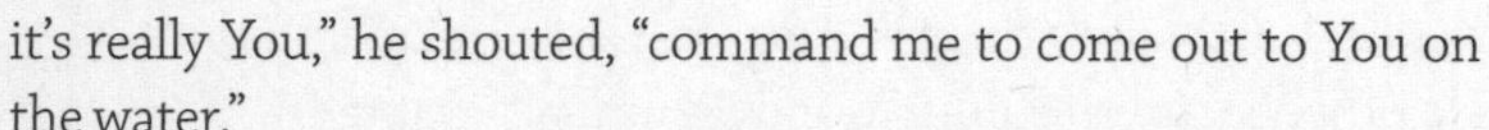

"Have courage!" Jesus shouted over the sound of the wind and the waves. "It's Me, don't be afraid."

Peter leaned closer and wiped the sea spray out of his eyes. "Lord, if it's really You," he shouted, "command me to come out to You on the water."

Jesus waved him on and said, "Come on."

The other disciples probably thought Peter was out of his mind as he started to step out of the boat and onto the water. They all watched to see what would happen to their brave but reckless friend. Peter put his foot out and made a hesitant step. Then another and another...till he was walking toward Jesus! On top of the water! With every step, Peter focused on only one thing—Jesus' smile.

Then something happened. Peter started thinking, "I can't believe I'm doing this! People can't walk on water!" He took his eyes off Jesus and started looking around. He saw how much the wind was blowing and the waves were crashing, and sure enough, Peter started to sink into the dark and swirling water.

"Lord," he cried as the water reached his shoulders, "save me!"

Jesus reached out, grabbed Peter's hand, and pulled him up. "Why did you doubt?" Jesus asked as He pulled His soggy friend to his feet. Then the two of them walked back to the boat—on the water! And just as they reached it, the wind stopped, and a beautiful moon-lit night settled on the Sea of Galilee.

All the other disciples stared at Peter, then at Jesus, and then at Peter again. They had seen Jesus do some amazing things before, but nothing quite like this.

Now they knew once and for all that Jesus wasn't only a great prophet or teacher or even a food multiplier. He truly was God's Son!

The Big Picture

What a wild day that had been for Peter! He helped Jesus feed thousands of people with just a small amount of food, he feared for his life in a terrible storm at sea, and then, to cap it all off, he walked on water! Peter wouldn't have traded that day for anything in the world because by the end of it, he knew that his best friend was far more than he had ever imagined. Now he knew that Jesus was God Himself wrapped up in a man!

18

"What Do You Say?" "Thank You": The Healed Lepers

Luke 17:11-19

As we've seen earlier, leprosy was a horrible disease that hurt people physically, emotionally, and socially. During Jesus' time, men and women with this disease couldn't even live in town with their families but were forced to live outside the village, often in caves and under trees.

One day, ten lepers heard that Jesus was coming their way. Would they be able to work up the courage to ask Him for help? And what would He say to them if they did?

In this story, we see Jesus in action, we see people learning how to live by faith, and we see how one man received even more than he had hoped for.

"You go!" one leper whispered.

"No, you!" another responded.

"What if He tells us to go away?" asked a third.

"It won't be the first time someone's done that," another said.

The ten men with leprosy huddled together at the edge of the town. They knew they weren't allowed to go any farther because of their dreadful disease. And if they did venture into town, they needed to shout, "Stay away! Unclean! Unclean!" to let everyone know they were sick. No one wanted to come close to these guys, so they reasoned that Jesus wouldn't either.

"Look," one said, pointing his bony finger toward the center of town. "There He is, our one hope for getting better."

"It's now or never," another added. "Here goes!"

All ten of them took a deep breath and then started shouting. "Jesus, Master, don't turn us away! Be kind to us! Please help us!"

When Jesus saw them, He could tell right away that they had leprosy. He said to them, "Go find the Jewish priest and show yourselves to him." Then Jesus continued on His way.

"Show ourselves to the priest?" they asked themselves as they looked at each other. They were confused.

One of them spoke up. "I thought people showed themselves to the priest *after* they were healed. Isn't that what Moses commanded?"

"But we're not healed yet!" another said. "What do we do? No priest is going to want to see us."

As the lepers considered what to do, one of them said, "I think we should do as He says. He told us to show ourselves to the priest, so that's what we should do."

They all nodded solemnly to one another and turned toward the synagogue. As they started their journey, something strange started to happen. At first their movements were the same as always—slow and painful. But then slowly, almost like a wave washing over their bodies, the pain that was in their feet and legs began to go away. Their arms felt stronger, and their breathing was easier. The painful scabs on their faces and hands began disappearing. They looked at one another and could see that something wonderful was happening! They were being healed!

As they continued their journey, their strength was restored, and they started leaping and jumping for the first time in months. Some

whirled around and danced. They laughed and shouted and started running. "Let's go show ourselves to the priest!" they shouted.

As they danced, leaped, and ran through the narrow street, one of the former lepers stopped.

He was from Samaria—an area that Jews tried to avoid. As the others continued up the street, they didn't notice him turning around and looking back at Jesus. He quickly retraced his steps until he caught up to Jesus and was face-to-face with the one who had healed him. Jesus stopped when He saw him, and the man who had been a leper knelt down and bowed low with his face to the ground.

Then he looked up and started thanking and praising Jesus for what He had just done.

Jesus looked at this young man who was good as new, and He said, "There were ten who were healed—where are the other nine? Are you the only one who came back to give thanks? I'm glad you returned, but you can go now. Because you believed, you've been made well."

The man got up, smiled at Jesus one more time, and went on his way. He had been healed, but even more importantly, his thankfulness had brought him close to Jesus.

The Big Picture

God has blessed us with so many things. Even when we're going through hard times, it's always important to be thankful to Him for all His goodness, kindness, and care. Think of three things you're thankful for right now, and tell God how much you appreciate what He's done.

Enter into His gates with thanksgiving,
And into His courts with praise.
Be thankful to Him, and bless His name (Psalm 100:4).

19

On the Road Again: Blind Bartimaeus

Mark 10:46-52

When Jesus walked on the earth, people quickly noticed that something about Him was unique. He loved the people whom everyone else rejected, He confronted the religious leaders who were misleading the crowd, and He healed the people who seemed to have no hope. One guy Jesus met had to try a little harder in order to get healed, but he found out soon enough that the result was worth all of his effort.

Bartimaeus walked to his normal spot on what he thought was going to be a normal day. He plopped down by the side of the road, adjusted his cloak, and got as comfortable as he could get sitting in the dirt by the side of the road to Jericho. Bart had been blind for years, and now that he was grown up, he had to sit by the road and beg for money so he could buy food. *Bar* meant "son of," and Timaeus was his dad's name, so Bartimaeus didn't even have a real name of his own. He was just "son of Tim." But as he had done with so many other things in his life that hadn't turned out the way he had hoped, Bartimaeus made the best of his situation and sat by the side of the road with his little bowl, hoping someone would put some money in. He was glad he lived with the Jews because God had often told them to take care of people who were poor.

It was a dry, dusty day, so Bart hoped there wouldn't be too many horses going by. The dust from their hooves made him cough and sneeze, and by the end of the afternoon, it also made him smell funny. He was just hoping for a nice, peaceful day.

Bartimaeus had sat there for some time when suddenly he heard voices—a lot of them. He could tell the people were coming from Jericho toward him. "Oh, great," he said, bracing himself. "Here comes the dust." But he also knew that with a lot of people coming, he had a chance to make some money.

The voices got closer. He cleared his throat. "Here ya go—blind guy here!" he shouted. "A chance to do a good deed! Remember what God says about taking care of the poor—that it's a good idea! Proverbs 14:21 says that people who have mercy on the poor will be blessed!"

A couple of grumpy guys strode over to Bart. "Keep it down, you nincompoop!" the first guy yelled. "Can't you see who's coming?"

"Well, actually..." Bart started to answer.

"It's the great prophet, Jesus. Mind your manners!" the guy said.

"Jesus?" Bartimaeus thought. "I've heard of Him! He's more than a prophet. He walked on water, He calmed a storm, He fed 5000 people, and He's healed people!" Bartimaeus hesitated. "You don't suppose..." he thought. "I wonder..."

Soon the crowd was right in front of him, so Bartimaeus took a deep breath and started shouting. "Jesus! Jesus! Son of David! Help me out here! Don't turn away!"

This made even more people mad at Bart. "Keep it down! Can't you see we've got a parade going on here?"

"Well, actually..." Bart started again, but the people kept interrupting.

"This guy is very important, and He certainly doesn't have time for a beggar sitting by the side of the road! So zip it!"

The more the people tried to make Bartimaeus be quiet, the louder he shouted. Now he had to shout over the crowd *and* over the people who were trying to shut him up.

"Jesus! I'm serious! Over here! Help me out here!"

Suddenly Jesus stopped and looked over to where the voice was coming from. He spotted Bartimaeus and said, "Go get that guy and bring him over here."

The same people who had been telling Bart to shut up suddenly put big cheesy smiles on their faces. They bowed down and made a path for the blind beggar. "Come, come, my friend. Jesus is calling you!" Talk about phonies.

Bart threw off his coat and scrambled over to Jesus like a kid whose father had just walked through the front door.

Jesus greeted Bartimaeus and looked intently at him. "What do you want Me to do for you?" Jesus asked.

Without hesitation Bartimaeus answered "Oh, Lord, I'd sure love to see again."

Jesus smiled and said, "Look what your faith has done for you."

Immediately Bart's eyes were completely healed, and he could see everything clearly. The very first thing he saw was Jesus' face. As he looked around, Bart realized there were a lot more people than he'd expected.

He saw the sunlight for the first time since he could remember. And Jericho's walls and the gates and the palm trees. He looked down. He saw his hands and feet. He was a lot taller than he remembered. He thought for a moment.

Jesus smiled and said, "Go your way."

"Go my way?" Bartimaeus thought. "I don't have any other way but the way You're going!"

So Bartimaeus left his little spot, his bowl, and his old sightless life. He walked with Jesus now.

The Big Picture

Bartimaeus was a guy with no sight and no name. But when he heard that Jesus was coming by, Bart did the one thing he could do—he called for help. Even when the others told him to be quiet, he kept calling. He believed in Jesus enough to cry out even if that meant making a fool of himself. That's what impressed Jesus. And that's why Bartimaeus was healed. He knew Jesus was the Son of God, and Bartimaeus wasn't going to let anybody talk him out of a miracle.

20

You're Not Who We Were Expecting: Jesus, the Unlikely Hero

Matthew 20:28

We know that Jesus was the greatest hero in the whole world. It's hard to imagine even though He is equal with God the Father, He left all the wonder of heaven and lived and walked on the earth and experienced life just the way we do. Jesus wasn't born in a big, beautiful bedroom, but in a stable. And He didn't live in a palace in Jerusalem, but in a small house with His family in a little town called Nazareth. He went to school, got dirty, and probably even scraped His knee or got stung by a wasp on occasion. And maybe this was the reason so many people in His day couldn't believe Jesus really was the Son of God. He seemed so...normal! But as people took a better look, many of them started to realize that Jesus was exactly who He said He was—the Savior, the Son of God.

Yes, when Jesus walked on the earth about 2000 years ago, He looked like an average Jew. That's why most of the Jewish people didn't believe that He was God's Son, the King of the world. They were waiting for a king like David—a warrior who would lead a revolution against the Roman Empire and set Israel free.

When the Jews read the Old Testament, they saw that the Messiah (God's chosen one) was going to come, rule in power, and set all the people free. So when Jesus came, He wasn't what the people were expecting. They wanted a military ruler, but Jesus spoke of love, forgiveness, and a different kind of kingdom—the kingdom of God. He didn't meet their expectations, so a lot of the people reasoned that Jesus couldn't possibly be the chosen one.

Even one of His disciples couldn't believe it was Him. "Isn't the chosen one supposed to come from Bethlehem? This guy's from Nazareth! And I don't see anywhere in the Bible that anything good comes from Nazareth." Check it out in John 1:45-46. (If he'd done his homework, he would have found out that Jesus really did come out of Bethlehem.)

But Jesus and His Father in heaven knew that we needed something far greater than a military king to lead us. We needed someone to restore our broken relationship with God. Starting with Adam and Eve, none of us have been perfect, so we weren't able to be close to a perfect God. God sent Jesus to come and take our place and our punishment and open the way back to the Father. Jesus is like a bridge leading us back to the Father.

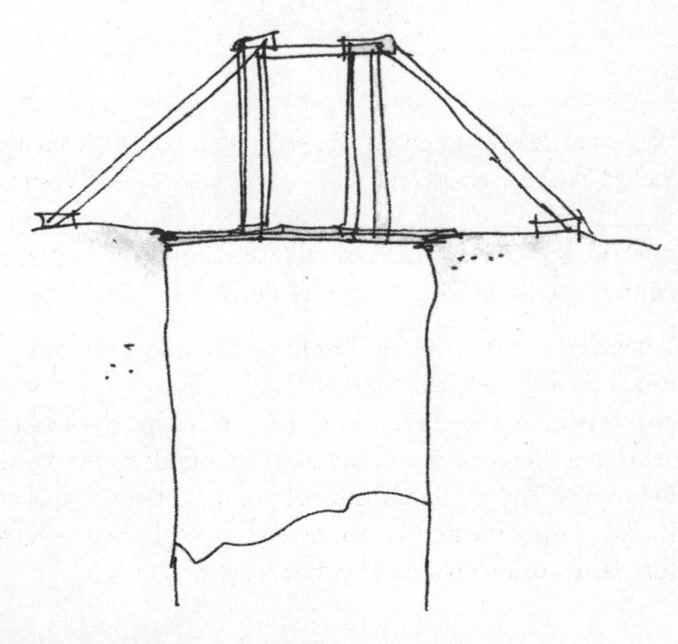

Someday Jesus will return and rule in righteousness, power, and love. But until then, we should get to know Him, obey Him, read His Word, and talk to Him every day through prayer.

Then, day by day, we'll start to look like our favorite unusual Bible hero, Jesus Himself!

More Great Harvest House Books by Sandy Silverthorne

The Awesome Book of Bible Stories for Kids

Sandy Silverthorne pairs biblical accounts with contemporary technology and culture. The result is a hilarious and informative blend of Bible lessons and modern-day applications. You'll instantly relate to Bible characters and eternal truths presented from a twenty-first-century kid's perspective.

The Awesome Book of Bible Facts

A beautiful full-color storybook, first Bible dictionary, and gold mine of fascinating facts all in one. This large hardback book is packed with amazing information, incredible cut-away diagrams, hundreds of illustrations, and short, easy explanations that you will love.

101 Awesome Bible Facts for Kids

Each entry in this 144-page pocket-size fact book includes an interesting statistic, a helpful definition, or some other noteworthy morsel of data from the Old or New Testament as well as a playful cartoon illustration. These interesting facts will help you become a Bible expert in no time!

One-Minute Mysteries and Brain Teasers

Return of the One-Minute Mysteries and Brain Teasers

Mind-Boggling One-Minute Mysteries and Brain Teasers

Your entire family will be astonished and stumped by these interactive mysteries. In brief paragraphs and black-and-white illustrations, Sandy joins John Warner in presenting puzzles with logical, "aha" answers that require thinking outside the box. Clues and answers are included in separate sections. Hours of wholesome entertainment are practically guaranteed!